TECHNIQUES
of the
WORLD'S GREAT
PHOTOGRAPHERS

TECHNIQUES
of the
WORLD'S GREAT PHOTOGRAPHERS

PHAIDON

Contributors
Brian Coe
David Allison
Amy Bedik
Terry Binns
Patrice Danielle
Colin Ford
Philippe Garner
Robert Hershkowitz
Waldemar Januszczak
Ian Jeffrey
Rupert Martin
Terence Pepper

A QED BOOK

Published by
Phaidon Press Limited
Littlegate House
St Ebbe's Street
Oxford OX1 1SQ

ISBN 0 7148 2187 X

Filmset in Great Britain by
Oliver Burridge and Company Limited,
Crawley, Sussex
Colour origination in Hong Kong by
Hong Kong Graphic Arts Service
Printed in Italy by Legatoria Editoriale
Giovanni Olivotto

This book was designed and produced by
QED Publishing Limited
32 Kingly Court, London W1

Art director Alastair Campbell
Production director Edward Kinsey
Senior Editor Kathy Rooney
Editor Nicola Thompson
Designer Clive Hayball
Editorial Victoria Funk, Catherine Carpenter,
Julian Mannering
Artwork Dennis Lloyd Thompson
Illustrators Brett Breckon, David Mallott,
David Staples
Picture Research Linda Proud, Ellie Player

Editor's note: As a useful cross-reference, the
names of photographers featured elsewhere in
the book are given in small capitals on their
first mention in a section.

Contents

C. HENTSCHEL SC.

"Photography appears to be an easy activity; in fact, it is a varied and ambiguous process in which the only common denominator among its practitioners is their instrument."
Henri Cartier-Bresson

Introduction

The history of photography is as much a story of technological development as of aesthetic or artistic concerns. The many routes which photography has followed in the last 150 years have all been the result of experiments and innovation – chemical, mechanical and technological. Practical photography began in 1839 with the publication of two quite different methods of recording optical images by chemical means. The first to be announced, although not the first to be published, was devised by LOUIS JACQUES MANDE DAGUERRE (1789–1851), and evolved from an impractical process developed by Nicéphore Niépce in the 1820s. Niépce and Daguerre worked together from 1829 until the former's death in 1833, trying to improve the original method which involved exposing bitumen-covered pewter plates in the camera for up to eight hours.

The daguerreotype process was announced in January 1839, but details were not released until August, after a government pension had been negotiated for Daguerre and Niépce's son. Daguerreotypes were made on silvered copper plates, highly polished and sensitized to light by exposure to iodine vapour, which produced a layer of silver iodide on the plate's surface. After several minutes exposure in the camera, the plate was 'developed' by vapour from heated mercury. The image

Nicéphore Niépce *(left)* made the earliest surviving photographic image *(below)*. It shows the view from his window at Gras. Taken in about 1826, it is a direct positive which was fixed on a pewter plate.

One of the problems of the daguerreotype was that if it was looked at from straight in front of it, the image appeared as a negative *(1)*. If looked at from the right, the image appeared half positive and half negative *(2)*. The wholly positive image *(3)* was only visible if viewed from the left.

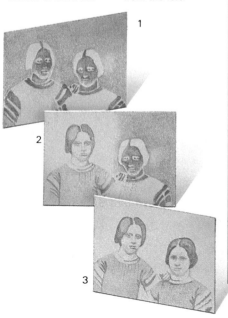

The daguerreotype process This was the earliest successful photographic process and it produced a direct positive image. First, a silvered copper plate was buffed *(1)* to achieve a fine polish.

The plate was now exposed in the camera. The exposure produced a latent image which was not visible. To develop the image, the plate was again held in a box over mercury vapour, made by heating mercury over a spirit lamp *(3)*. The mercury reacted with the silver iodide that had been exposed to light to form a visible image. Where the mercury was attached to the plate, it was shiny and bright, while the silver iodide remained dark where no light had touched the plate.

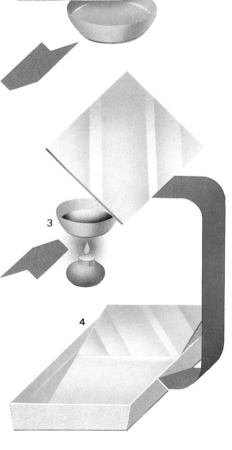

To make the polished plate sensitive to light, it was then iodized *(2)*. The silver side of the plate was placed over a bowl of iodine crystals inside a wooden box. The vapour from the iodine reacted with the silver to make silver iodide – a light-sensitive compound.

To fix the image, Daguerre soaked the plate in a strong salt solution *(4)*. After a discovery by Sir John Herschel, this was replaced with sodium thiosulphate, usually known as hypo. The fixing agent dissolved away any of the silver iodide that had not been exposed to light and therefore remained unchanged. The original bare metal plate was then revealed as black to form the dark areas of the picture.

This daguerreotype *(right)* is a self-portrait by an amateur British photographer, George Shaw. It was taken with a quarter plate camera in the 1850s.

was then 'fixed' by removing the unused silver iodide, initially with a strong salt solution, but later with 'hypo', a sodium thiosulphate solution.

As first announced, the daguerreotype process had several drawbacks being very insensitive and making portraiture almost impossible because of long exposure times. The image was fragile and could be damaged with a touch; thus each picture was unique and if more than one copy was required, a number of originals had to be taken. The sensitivity of the process was greatly improved in 1840 with John Goddard's discovery that exposure to bromine vapour as well as iodine made the plate faster, and Antoine Claudet's discovery the following year of a similar effect with chlorine. Hippolyte Fizeau's discovery in 1840 that treating the developed and fixed plate with gold chloride solution not only improved the contrast of the image but also greatly strengthened its resistance to abrasion, removed another of the objections. In 1840 too, Josef Petzval created a four element lens design with a maximum aperture of f.3.6, 16 times faster than the simple lenses then in use. These chemical and optical improvements made portraiture much easier, and from 1841 the daguerreotype process came into widespread use.

Another drawback, the uniqueness of the image, was inherent in the daguerreotype process and doomed it to extinction within two decades. In that period, it was used primarily for commercial portraiture, although still-life, architectural and landscape subjects were also tackled.

Modern photography evolved from a process devised by WILLIAM HENRY FOX TALBOT (1800–1877) who, in 1834, began experiments in sensitizing paper to light. By impregnating paper with silver chloride which darkened when light fell on it, Talbot was able to make 'negative' images of leaves, lace and so on, which he 'fixed' by treating the paper with a strong salt solution. In 1835, using these negative images as originals, he produced positive copies on his sensitized paper. In the summer of the same year he placed his 'photogenic drawing' paper in small cameras and made negative images of his home, Lacock Abbey in Wiltshire, England. When he heard of Daguerre's announcement in 1839, Talbot immediately published details of his own method, which was the first publication ever of a practical photographic process.

Like the daguerreotype, Talbot's photogenic drawing process suffered from a lack of sensitivity, with exposures of an hour or more in the camera required, but in September 1840 Talbot discovered that an invisible, or latent, image was produced by

9

Photogenic drawing Invented by William Henry Fox Talbot, this process produced negative images of lace, leaves and other objects when they were placed on paper which had been specially prepared. A good quality writing paper was dipped into a weak salt solution *(1)*. The paper was then dried and one side of the paper was made light-sensitive by coating it with a solution of silver nitrate *(2)*. Before the paper could be used, it had to be washed in a strong salt solution *(3)*. The paper was then exposed, wet or dry, and the image appeared, with the parts which were exposed to light turning black. The image was fixed *(4)* originally with a strong salt solution, but later with hypo.

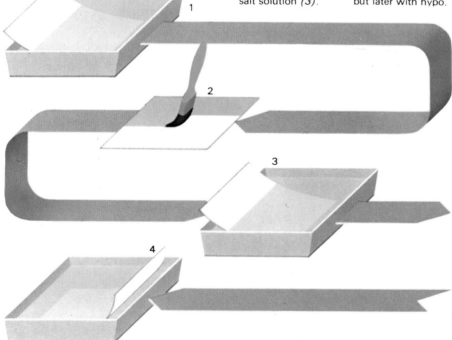

a brief exposure, and that this image could be revealed by a chemical process of development. Talbot patented and published his new process in 1841 under the name calotype, although the 'honorary' name Talbotype was also used, especially on commercial prints.

While it lacked the extreme definition of the daguerreotype, the calotype gave perfectly adequate sharpness, especially since the prints were usually of larger format than the normal daguerreotype. The warm reddish-brown image colour of the calotype was preferred by many to the cold, neutral tone of the daguerreotype, and the process was widely used in England and France in the 1840s, although it reached no significant use in the United States, where the daguerreotype reigned supreme. The easy duplication by printing from the calotype negative made the sale and distribution of photographs possible on a much larger scale than the daguerreotype. The majority of calotypes were of architectural or landscape subjects; for commercial portraiture, the daguerreotype remained popular.

To facilitate the printing of the paper negative, Talbot recommended that after

10

The salt print
Making a salt print involves a process which is virtually the same as Talbot's photogenic drawing process. Good quality writing paper was dipped into a salt solution *(1)* and then floated on a bath of silver nitrate *(2)*. The paper was then exposed by contact with the negative until a strong enough image appeared. The final image was then washed *(3)*, toned *(4)* and fixed *(5)* in a solution of hypo.

The calotype process The calotype was the first photograph that was printed on to paper from a negative. Similar to the photographic drawing process, the first step was to brush one side of a piece of good writing paper with a silver nitrate solution *(1)*. This was dried and then gently placed in a solution of potassium iodide *(2)* so that silver iodide was formed. When the paper was needed it was floated on a bath of gallo-nitrate of silver *(3)*. It was then put in a dark slide and exposed. The latent (hidden) image was developed by washing with gallo-nitrate of silver *(4)*. Finally, the print was washed *(5)* and fixed *(6)* in a bath of hypo.

Seascape *(1850s)* *(below)* Le Gray made this image by combining two negatives achieved using the wet collodion on glass process. It was one of a series of large albumen prints made using this process.

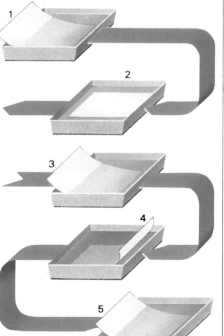

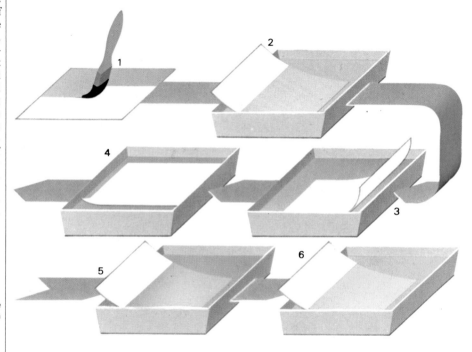

processing it should be waxed to make it translucent. Taking this a step further, in 1851 the French photographer, GUSTAVE LE GRAY (1820–1862) proposed an improvement by which the paper was waxed before being sensitized. This improved not only the definition of the negative, but also its keeping properties. While calotype paper was best used soon after sensitizing, waxed paper could be kept for weeks before use, a useful feature for the travel-ling photographer. The main drawback of this process was reduced sensitivity, with long exposure times required, but the waxed paper negative process was still used extensively in the 1850s, mostly for architectural and landscape photography. In 1850, an improved printing paper was introduced by Louis-Desiré Blanquart-Evrard in which, before sensitizing, the paper was coated with a thin layer of albumen (egg white), giving it a smooth,

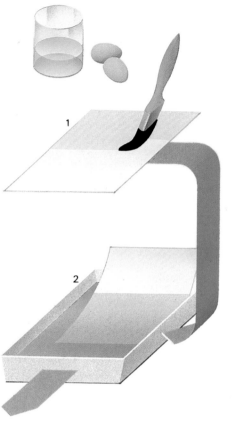

William Henry Fox Talbot's home was Lacock Abbey in Wiltshire, England. He took many photographs of the Abbey and made this image of the South Aspect in 1848. It is one of the many calotypes made by Talbot which can now be seen at the museum at Lacock Abbey.

Le Gray's waxed paper process This process produced a much finer image than Talbot's calotype. A high quality paper was put on a heated, silvered copper plate and pure wax was then rubbed into it *(1)*. Any excess wax was removed *(2)* by ironing the paper between blotting paper. The paper was then soaked in an iodizing solution made from potassium fluoride, potassium cyanide, potassium iodide, rice water and lactose *(3)*. The paper was dried and could be kept for up to 14 days before use. The paper was sensitized *(4)* by floating it briefly on a silver nitrate solution. Then it was dried and exposed. To develop the image, the paper was soaked in a solution of gallic acid *(5)*. Finally, the image was fixed *(6)* and washed in hypo like other prints.

11

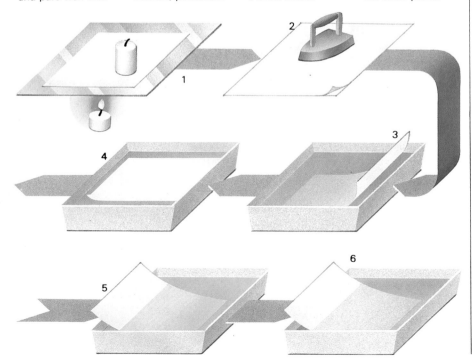

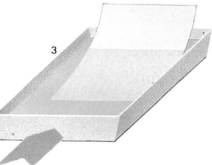

The albumen print process Louis Desiré Blanquart-Evrard introduced the albumen process in 1850 and it became very popular. The process was fairly simple. First, a sheet of good quality, thin writing paper was coated with a layer of fresh albumen (egg white) *(1)*. The paper became sensitized after it had been dipped into a silver nitrate solution *(2)*. After exposure to a negative, the image was fixed in a bath of hypo *(3)*. Sometimes a small amount of gold chloride was added to the fixing bath. This gave the final print a much deeper tone than was obtained using pure hypo. The albumen print was quite smooth and glossy, producing an image that was much more detailed than a salt print, for example.

slightly lustrous surface which gave improved definition of the image. Albumen paper soon replaced the uncoated paper used in the calotype process, and remained in general use almost until the end of the century.

The limited transparency of the paper negative meant long printing times, and even the waxed paper process imposed a limit on the amount of definition that the negative could resolve. Glass seemed to be the ideal medium, but being impermeable it would have to be coated with a light-sensitive layer. The first practical glass plate process was published by Abel Niepce de Saint Victor, cousin of Nicéphore Niépce, in 1847 who proposed the use of an albumen coating on the glass plate, sensitized in a similar way to the calotype negative. These albumen plates, although very insensitive, gave a very high resolution of detail, were easy to use, and for many years were popular with landscape and architectural photographers, for whom long exposures were of little consequence.

The first glass plate process to enjoy widespread use was the wet collodion process, first published by Frederick Scott Archer in March 1851. Archer's process used the newly-discovered collodion — a solution of guncotton (pyroxylin) in ether and alcohol which also contained potassium iodide. A small amount of this solution was poured into the centre of a glass plate and quickly spread over it by tilting the plate towards each corner in turn. The collodion coating dried quickly and, while still tacky, the plate was plunged into a bath of silver nitrate sol-

ution to sensitize it. The drained but still moist plate was then put into a plate-holder, exposed immediately, and processed without delay.

The collodion plate was capable of high definition and was admirably suited for printing on the new albumen paper. A major problem, however, was the need to prepare the plate just before exposure which required a portable darkroom to be carried by the photographer when work-

This engraving shows a wet collodion photographer at work in the 1850s. Like many wet collodion photographers, he has an assistant to help him. The wet collodion photographic process was quite complicated and an extra pair of hands were useful. The glass plates had to be coated with collodion in the dark and exposed while still wet.

12

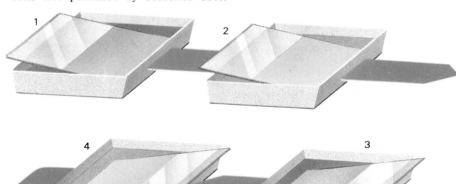

Frederick Scott Archer (1813–1857) was the first to show the use of wet collodion on glass negatives in a practical way. He perfected the process in March 1851.

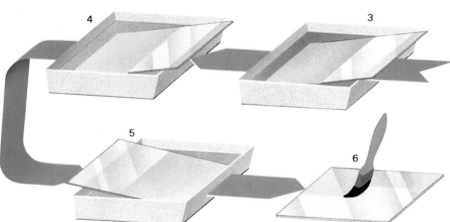

The wet collodion process Collodion is a soluble guncotton (pyroxylin) dissolved in a mixture of ether and alcohol. The first stage of this process was to dissolve bromide and iodide salts in collodion. A clean glass plate was then coated with this solution (1). When dry the plate was immersed in a silver nitrate solution (2). The silver nitrate reacts with the collodion to form either silver iodide or silver bromo-iodide which both make the glass much more sensitive. The wet glass plate was exposed and then immediately covered with a developer (3) to process it. The negative was then fixed in a strong solution of hypo (4) and washed (5) as in other processes. Finally, the negative was given a protective covering of spirit varnish (6).

A variety of photographic prints are made by contact printing from a glass negative. This involves pressing paper to a negative while exposing them both to light.

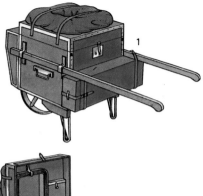

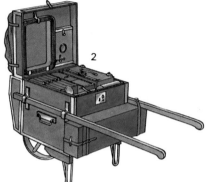

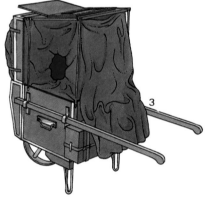

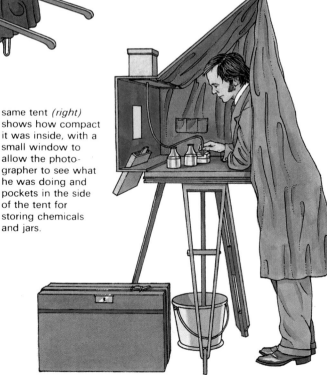

Photographers who used the wet collodion process were obliged to carry a great deal of heavy equipment with them if they were working out of doors. One of the most popular forms of dark-tent that these photographers used was called the 'perambulator' or 'wheelbarrow'. It was extremely compact and easy to wheel when it was folded *(1)*. All the glass plates and chemicals required were stored in small compartments which were revealed when the lid was opened *(2)*. This lid became the back of the dark-tent when it was assembled *(3)*.

This engraving carried by the *Illustrated London News* shows Roger Fenton's photographic van which he took to the Crimea. Fenton photographed Marcus Sparling, his assistant, sitting on the box before their journey.

Portable dark-tents were made by many manufacturers in the 1860s in response to the huge demand from photographers who used the wet collodion process. They needed to take their darkrooms, complete with chemicals, with them if they were to photograph successfully out of doors. One of the earliest types of portable dark-tents that could be folded up and carried like a suitcase was W W Rouch's of 1862. The section of the same tent *(right)* shows how compact it was inside, with a small window to allow the photographer to see what he was doing and pockets in the side of the tent for storing chemicals and jars.

ing away from home. Some photographers, like the Briton ROGER FENTON (1819–1869) had horsedrawn vans; others carried collapsible tents which were erected on site. The outfit of a travelling photographer now had to include not only a large stand camera, tripod and plate-holders, but also a dark tent, glass plates, chemicals, dishes, glassware and even a supply of water if this was not available on site. Despite this, photographers managed to travel all over the world: up mountains, like the Bisson brothers, Louis-Auguste and Auguste-Rosalie, or Samuel Bourne (1834–1912), or through the heat of the desert, like FRANCIS FRITH (1822–1898) whose collodion boiled due to the intense heat.

With very few exceptions, all prints from a wet collodion negative were made by contact printing which meant that the final print was the same size as the negative. If a large print was needed, a large glass plate had to be coated and processed, using a suitably large camera. Plates up to 16 × 20in were in regular use, and even larger sizes were not uncommon. Most exterior photography was carried out with whole-plates (6.5 × 8.5in) or 10 × 8in plates, although smaller sizes were also popular, especially with amateurs.

The wet collodion process was appreciably faster than the calotype, although not dramatically so, with exposures for well-lit exteriors running into tens of seconds. Action-stopping and instantaneous exposures were not practical except under very special circumstances, and, for this reason, photographs of busy streets appear empty except for a few ghostly passers-by who paused long enough to be registered on the plate.

Camera design in the 1840s and 1850s was mostly of the sliding-box type which consisted of two wooden boxes, one sliding within the other, one fitted with the lens and the other holding the focusing screen and plate or paper holder. After the mid-1850s, folding bellows cameras became increasingly popular for outdoor photography as they were lighter and less bulky than the sliding-box type. A substantial amount of general landscape and architectural photography of the period was done with simple achromatic lenses with maximum apertures of f.16 or less, frequently stopped down to f.45, f.64 or even smaller. Indoor portraiture, on the other hand, was usually carried out with four-element lenses of the type designed by Josef Max Petzval. The f.3.6 aperture of the Petzval lens made the best use of the reduced daylight in the studio, and its limited field depth and covering power were not serious disadvantages for portraits, although they did rule the lens out

13

for exterior work. From the mid-1860s, the Rapid Rectilinear and Aplanatic lenses, which used a pair of achromatic lenses with a maximum aperture of f.8 gave good covering power and resolution and these quickly became popular for general photography. Cameras were not normally fitted with shutters; exposures were made by removing and replacing the lens cap, and because of long exposure times, a tripod or studio stand was needed to support the camera.

The next major change in the photographic process came in 1871 with the publication of a dry plate process by Dr Richard Leach Maddox. The virtues of the wet collodion negative were to some extent off-set by the problem of having to coat plates on the spot; plates could be prepared in advance by the albumen process, but exposures from the plates were very slow.

Maddox was inspired to find a substitute for collodion since his health had been affected by ether fumes. He found that by mixing a solution of melted gelatin with a halide such as cadmium bromide and silver nitrate, an 'emulsion' of silver bromide in gelatin was formed which

14

could be spread on a plate or paper and dried. The dried gelatin plates kept their properties for some time. As first published, Maddox's formula was not very practical, and offered no great advantages over the wet collodion process, but improvements soon followed. Richard Kennett of London marketed ready-made emulsions which he heat-dried and sold as a 'pellicle' for reconstituting and coating by the photographer. Plates made from these emulsions were noticeably faster than freshly made ones, and in 1878 Charles Bennett concluded that heating the emulsions 'ripened' them and greatly increased their speed.

Commercial manufacture of the improved gelatin dry plates began on a large scale in the late 1870s, and within a very few years the wet collodion process was virtually obsolete. The new dry plates had many virtues. They could be made in consistent batches by manufacturers, which

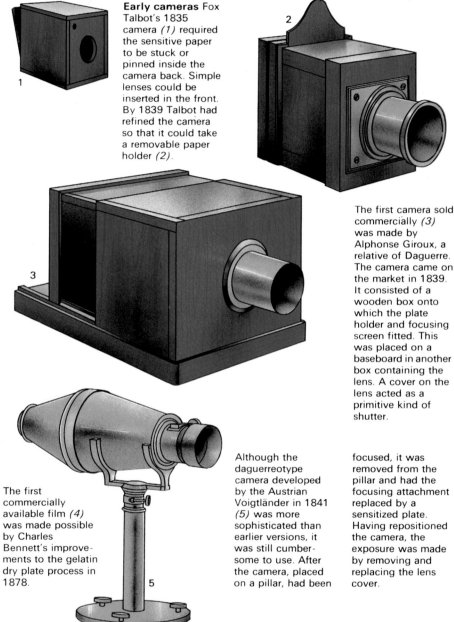

Early cameras Fox Talbot's 1835 camera *(1)* required the sensitive paper to be stuck or pinned inside the camera back. Simple lenses could be inserted in the front. By 1839 Talbot had refined the camera so that it could take a removable paper holder *(2)*.

The first camera sold commercially *(3)* was made by Alphonse Giroux, a relative of Daguerre. The camera came on the market in 1839. It consisted of a wooden box onto which the plate holder and focusing screen fitted. This was placed on a baseboard in another box containing the lens. A cover on the lens acted as a primitive kind of shutter.

The first commercially available film *(4)* was made possible by Charles Bennett's improvements to the gelatin dry plate process in 1878.

Although the daguerreotype camera developed by the Austrian Voigtländer in 1841 *(5)* was more sophisticated than earlier versions, it was still cumbersome to use. After the camera, placed on a pillar, had been focused, it was removed from the pillar and had the focusing attachment replaced by a sensitized plate. Having repositioned the camera, the exposure was made by removing and replacing the lens cover.

The dry plate process
A major disadvantage with the wet plate process was that the plates had to be prepared on site. The gelatin dry plate negative soon replaced the wet collodion method as it could be made in advance. A glass plate was coated *(1)* with a gelatin emulsion

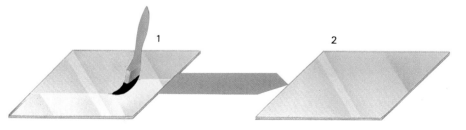

The sliding box camera *(6)* became popular during the 1840s and 1850s, and remained so throughout the nineteenth century. The front box with the lens was fitted onto the baseboard. On this, a second and smaller box slid into the first. The plate holder or focusing screen was inserted along vertical grooves in the back of the smaller box.

The sliding box camera was very large and its shape awkward. However, around 1855, a folding version *(7, 8)* was developed. This compact model was, of course, popular with itinerant photographers. The lens panel and plate holder could be removed and then the sides of the camera could be folded flat.

This early wet plate camera *(10)* had a removable focusing screen. The plate holder was inserted along grooves in the back of the camera.

The first single lens reflex camera *(9)* was developed as early as 1861 by Thomas Sutton.

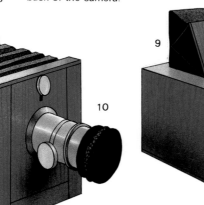

eliminated the need to carry a portable dark tent around, and they would keep their properties for months. But the biggest advantage was their sensitivity. Dry plates could be made in a range of speeds to suit different needs, and exposures could be reduced to fractions of a second, making action photography possible. All of these advantages meant that the dry plate greatly extended the range of subjects which the photographer could tackle.

Meanwhile, the design of cameras was being radically altered. In the 1880s, hand cameras with built-in shutters and view-finders appeared for the first time, and add-on shutters were supplied for use with stand cameras. To enable the photographer to assess correct exposure from a combination of factors such as time of day, season, weather, subject, type of plate and so on, a variety of exposure calculating and measuring gadgets appeared.

As the gelatin emulsion could be applied to paper, a new generation of printing papers also appeared around 1880. One type were printing-out papers, which were printed in daylight in contact with the negative like the albumen papers which they soon began to replace. Others used gelatin-silver chloride emulsions – or 'gaslight' papers – which were given short exposures to artificial light followed by development. Such papers at last liberated the photographer from having to wait for fine weather before printing the negatives. The gelatin-silver bromide papers were very sensitive to light, which meant that they could be used for making enlargements by projecting the negative up to any size. This gave an important boost to the reduction of negative sizes, and by the turn of the century the most popular negative size for general photography was the $3\frac{1}{4} \times 4\frac{1}{4}$in quarter-plate.

Apart from the new gelatin-silver printing papers, at the end of the century there were several alternative printing processes available to the photographer. The platinum process, introduced in 1873 by William Willis, was based on the fact that iron salts change from the ferric to the ferrous form when exposed to light. Plain paper, treated with platinum chloride and ferric oxalate, was exposed to sunlight under a negative. The exposed paper was then treated with potassium oxalate solution, and pure platinum was deposited in the paper in proportion to the exposure. Platinum prints had a rich tonal range, and the image was completely permanent, unlike silver prints, which could be attacked by a variety of pollutants. The process was used extensively in the 1880s, 1890s and 1900s, but dramatic rises in the price of platinum made the process obsolete after the First World War.

15

instead of collodion to make the plate light-sensitive. This was made by mixing melted gelatin with a halide such as silver nitrate. The plate was then dried and stored away *(2)*. The gelatin emulsion never completely dried out. After exposure the image was fixed in a solution of hypo *(3)*. Finally, the negative was washed *(4)*.

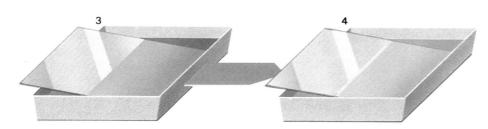

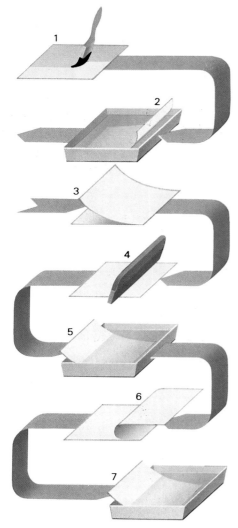

Another group of new printing methods were based on a discovery made in 1839 by Mungo Ponton that potassium bichromate alters when exposed to light. In 1852 Talbot discovered that gelatin treated with bichromate hardened on exposure to light, in proportion to exposure, and this principle was exploited in several later processes. If a bichromated layer of gelatin containing a pigment such as carbon black is exposed to light under a negative, it hardens most where light reaches it through those areas of the negative representing the shadows of the subject. The highlights of the picture, darkest in the negative, are the least hard. The exposed gelatin layer is washed in warm water and the unhardened gelatin and pigment washed away, leaving a positive image.

The carbon process was described by Alphonse Louis Poitevin in 1855, but was not taken up until it was improved by Joseph Wilson Swan in 1864. Carbon prints were permanent and could show most of the subtlety of a silver image, as well as being available in a wide variety of pigment colours. Carbon printing was used extensively in the production of commerical editions of photographs and for book illustration in the last quarter of the nineteenth century. A similar process used a coating of bichromated gum arabic instead of gelatin, and the gum-bichromate process was used in the 1890s and 1900s by 'impressionistic' photographers for the control over the final image it provided.

Carbon prints were made by contact from negatives of the same size, since they were printed in daylight. Thus if a large print was needed, a large negative had to be produced. In 1889 the discovery that bichromated gelatin in contact with a silver image was affected in the same way as when it was exposed to light was made by Howard Farmer. This phenomenon was used in Thomas Manly's ozobrome process in 1905. A bromide print, which could be an enlargement, was pressed into close contact with a bichromated carbon tissue soaked in a bleaching solution. As the silver image was bleached, the carbon tissue was selectively hardened and then processed as usual; the bromide print could be redeveloped and used again. Ozobrome, later also known as carbro, was used by many photographers for exhibition printing, and also formed the

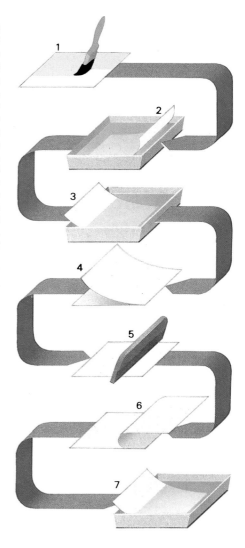

The carbon print Initially, a sheet of paper was coated *(1)* with a gelatin emulsion containing pigment of any colour. After plunging it into a solution of potassium bichromate *(2)*, to sensitize it, the paper was dried. Next exposure took place under a negative in a contact-printing frame. Daylight hardened the gelatin in inverse proportion to the density of the negative so that where the negative was darkest, the gelatin remained soft and unaltered. As the hardened

gelatin covered the top surface it was best to develop the print from the back. Therefore the paper was put face down onto another sheet, which had already been soaked in warm water *(3)*. The two sheets were then pressed together with a squeegee *(4)*. The two sheets were then soaked in warm water *(5)* so that after a short time the original sheet of paper could be peeled away *(6)*, leaving what had been the underside of the gelatin exposed. Any gelatin that had not been hardened was then

washed away in hot water *(7)*. The colour with which the paper had at first been pigmented formed the darkest colour on the print. By washing the unhardened gelatin

away down to the surface of the paper, the tones were exposed to reveal an image. One major disadvantage of this process was that the final image was reversed.

The ozobrome process A sheet of good quality paper was coated *(1)* with a gelatin emulsion containing coloured pigment. Next it was immersed in a potassium bichromate solution *(2)*. The pigmented paper was then bleached *(3)* and put into close contact with a silver bromide print in a printing frame *(4)*.

The two were squeegeed together *(5)* so that the bleached pigment paper reacted with the silver in the bromide print. The bromide print was then peeled away *(6)*. Any of the emulsion on the pigment paper that had not reacted was washed off in hot water to reveal the image *(7)*.

basis of several colour printing processes. The bromoil process, published by Piper and Wall in 1907, also used bromide prints. The print was bleached in a bichromating solution, which selectively hardened it, and was washed and fixed. The bleached print was pigmented by hand using greasy inks which 'took' in pro-

16

George Eastman (1854–1932) *(above)* was an American inventor and industrialist. By manufacturing his photographic inventions on a massive scale, he contributed greatly to the development of photography as a popular hobby. He invented a dry plate process and opened a factory to produce plates in 1880. Eastman was also responsible for the first Kodak camera and celluloid roll film he developed for it *(above right)*.

The Eastman-Walker roll holder *(above)* was the first roll-holder that was a commercial success. It was devised jointly by George Eastman and William Walker who was Eastman's camera manufacturer in Rochester, New York. Eastman invented his Eastman negative paper as a substitute for glass plate negatives. Together, the two men then designed a holder for rolls of this new paper. The paper was wound onto a wooden core and kept taut by a spring mechanism so that it was held flat in the focal plane. The roll-holder was used instead of a plate-holder and it could be fitted to any conventional stand camera.

portion to the original image. The considerable amount of control over the final image attracted many exhibition photographers to the bromoil process.

The general adoption of the gelatin dry plate, from the late 1870s on, was the last radical change in the basic chemistry of photography which has remained essentially the same ever since, although there have been many improvements and refinements. The early photographic plates were all sensitive only to blue and violet light and did not respond to any degree to the other colours of the spectrum. In 1873 Dr H W Vogel discovered that the addition of certain dyes to the sensitive layer of the plate could extend its sensitivity to other colours. This discovery was applied to the new gelatin dry plates, and in 1882 the first isochromatic – or orthochromatic – plates were introduced, sensitive to green as well as blue light. To counteract their excessive blue sensitivity, isochromatic plates were usually exposed through yellow filters. In 1884 Dr Vogel discovered a dye which further extended the sensitivity of the emulsion to orange. The first manufactured panchromatic plates, equally sensitive to all colours, were sold in 1906, but both blue-sensitive and isochromatic plates continued to be popular for 40 years.

Another important consequence of the dry processes was the development of roll film photography. George Eastman, one of the first to manufacture the new dry plates in the United States in 1879, looked for ways of popularizing photography. In 1885, with William Walker, he designed and marketed a roll holder which adapted the conventional plate camera to take a roll of negative paper 'film' of up to 48 exposures; the equivalent of this lightweight roll of paper in glass plates would have been an intolerable burden. In 1888 Eastman introduced a small box camera with an integral roll holder carrying a paper roll for 100 exposures 2.5in in diameter. His Kodak camera was backed up with a developing and printing service, and for the first time the photographer did not have to become involved in processing or have access to a darkroom.

The following year, 1889, Eastman introduced the first commercial transparent celluloid roll film for the Kodak camera. The first roll film cameras were darkroom loaded, but in 1895 Eastman adopted an invention by Samuel N Turner which used a black paper strip to which the film was attached, protecting it while it was loaded and unloaded, and bearing white exposure numbers which could be read through a red window in the back of the camera. Initially, the roll film cameras attracted new customers for photography, but soon

17

experienced photographers realized the advantages of the compact, lightweight cameras and as the roll film cameras and films improved in quality, more and more serious photographers adopted them. After the First World War, the plate camera began to decline in popularity except with professional users, and the trend was towards films and smaller negative formats.

Miniature plate cameras had become popular in the early years of the twentieth century, particularly those using the 'vest-pocket' format of 2 × 2.5in and a large variety of these small, pocketable plate cameras were sold before the First World War. The introduction of a range of new optical glasses in Jena in 1888 had led to the appearance of the first anastigmatic lenses which gave improved quality and led to the development of lenses with wider apertures, one of the first being the Zeiss Protar of 1890 with f.6.3 and f.4.5 apertures. The Zeiss Tessar lens of 1902 at first had a maximum aperture of f.5.5, but by 1907 f.4.5 and f.3.5 versions were introduced. New glasses developed in the 1940s allowed the four-element design of the Tessar to be extended to f.2.8 apertures after the Second World War. Ex-

tremely wide aperture lenses appeared in the 1920s, with the Ernemann Ernostar lens of f.2 aperture in 1923 increased to f.1.8 in 1925. These lenses were incorporated in the Ernemann Ermanox miniature plate camera in 1924.

Used with new, faster plates, these cameras for the first time permitted 'candid' photography in ordinary interiors, and photographers such as Erich Salomon (1866–1944) and Felix Man (born 1893)

Camera developments The first 35mm single lens reflex camera was the Ihagee Kine Exacta made in 1936. The 1937 model (1) had an improved focusing magnifier. The camera had a variable focal plane shutter.

1

used them with great success for reportage. From 1913 to 1924 a number of still cameras appeared using 35mm perforated film which had originally been introduced in the mid-1890s for new movie cameras but none made much of an impression on the market. Then, in 1925, Leitz introduced the Leica camera, based on a prototype developed by Oskar Barnack in 1913. The first Leica had a focal plane shutter with speeds from 1/25 to 1/500 per second, and, usually, an Elmar f.3.5 lens.

The precision of manufacture, and the high quality of the lens allied with its compact size, made it immediately popular, capable as it was of producing high quality 24 × 36mm negatives from which enlargements could be made. Improved models followed in the 1930s with interchangeable lenses, coupled rangefinders and faster shutter speeds, and the Leica was joined by the Zeiss Contax camera, with a similar specification. These two precision cameras, aided by the range of new films designed specifically for 35mm still photography in the 1930s, set the 35mm format on the way to its present pre-eminent position.

The appearance of the first Rolleiflex

18

2

3

4

When in 1925 Leica produced their 35mm camera (2), it became an instant success. The prototype had been made as early as 1913. The camera had shutter speeds which ranged from 1/25 to 1/500 of a second. The quality and precision of the camera and its lens added to its appeal. The first model was improved, but the 1925 version remains a classic which set the 35mm format on the road to the supremacy it still holds today.

In 1932 Zeiss Ikon produced the Contax camera in reaction to the Leica model. The 1934 model (4) had a coupled range-finder, separate optical viewfinder and had a shutter which had a slow speed range.

The twin lens reflex camera developed by Rolleiflex (3) in 1928 was a major advance which enabled many photographers, both professional and amateur, to get away from the large format plate camera. The Rolleiflex gave high optical and mechanical quality and took square negatives.

camera late in 1928 was another important development. The Rolleiflex revived the twin lens reflex camera design which had enjoyed a brief popularity around the turn of the century, but in the form of a compact roll film camera which took 2.25in square negatives. Of high mechanical and optical quality, it was an important influence in leading the advanced amateur and professional photographer away from the large format plate camera. After the Second World War, 2.25in square and 35mm became the principal formats for serious photography, and the single lens reflex camera, popularized in the 1950s in its modern miniature form, is now the almost exclusive working tool of amateur and professional photographers alike.

Colour photography today is the principal medium for most photographers. The first colour photograph was demonstrated in 1861 by James Clerk Maxwell, but practical methods of colour photography were not possible until the development of panchromatic emulsions around the turn of the century. The first commercially successful process was the Lumière Autochrome colour plate introduced in 1907.

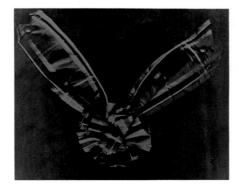

The first colour photograph was made in 1861 by James Clerk Maxwell using three colour separations.

The glass plates were covered with a mosaic of microscopic starch grains – dyed red, green and blue – and coated with a panchromatic emulsion which was exposed through the colour filters; the plate was then reversal-processed to give a colour positive. The plates were slow, requiring exposures of a second or more even in good light, and the irregular mosaic of filters could give a grainy, 'pointillist' effect. None the less, Autochrome was used by many leading photographers of the day in spite of – and even because of – its limitations, remaining on the market for almost 30 years. Other screen plates were produced using similar principles by manufacturers, but none was

The autochrome process The first stage was to mix powdered starch grains (1). The mixed powder was then poured (2) onto a glass plate covered with a tacky coating | The plate had to be passed through a machine-roller (3) to make the grains smooth and even. The plate was then sensitized (4) in a silver bromide emulsion. The plate was developed (5) then rinsed and, immersed in a reversal bath (6). The plate was reexposed to white light (7) when all the metallic silver had been washed away and then it had to be redeveloped in the original developer (8) Finally the plate was washed (9) and dried.

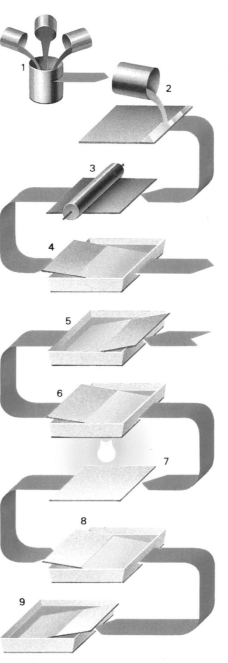

as successful as the Lumière product.

Various methods for producing three-colour prints or transparencies were in use from the beginning of the century. These required sets of separation negatives exposed through red, green, and blue filters using special colour cameras which made the exposures in quick succession, or simultaneously through complicated optical systems. The negatives were printed using carbon or carbro printing methods as three images coloured cyan, magenta, and yellow, and superimposed on one another in accurate register. One successful version, operated commercially in England in the 1930s, was Vivex. Alternatively, gelatin reliefs produced from the separation negatives were used to transfer dye images by printing in register. The Jos-Pe process of the 1920s, the Eastman wash-off relief process of the 1930s, and the Eastman dye transfer method of the 1940s all used this imbibition printing method.

Modern colour films date from the introduction of Kodachrome film in 1935 which was the first of the multiple-layer colour films in which the analysis and synthesis of colour took place within a single film. Introduced first for 16mm movies, Kodachrome film was sold for 35mm still photography from September 1936. Later that year, Agfacolor film appeared using a similar multilayer construction but with different processing methods. These transparency materials were followed by the Kodacolor process for colour prints from colour negatives, launched in 1942 in the United States. The wide range of modern colour materials have all evolved from these pioneering products.

Today's 400 ASA colour films are 11 million times more sensitive than Niépce's bitumen covered plate. In few art forms have technological and aesthetic concerns been more interdependent. The works by the world's great photographers depend not only on their own talents, but also on the equipment and processes which are at their disposal.

This 1935 Kodachrome film had 18 exposures and was the first multiple layer colour film. It was used for the increasingly popular 35mm | cameras.

19

THE PHOTOGRAPHERS

louis jacques mandé daguerre

French/1789–1851

"I have seized the light, I have arrested its flight."

Credit for the production of the earliest surviving photographic image must go, indubitably, to the French experimenter Joseph Nicéphore Niépce. The image in question, which researches have dated to 1826 or 1827, is a direct positive view, made on a sensitized pewter plate. This crude and indistinct achievement is nonetheless a remarkable creation, perhaps the most magical of all early photographic images. Niépce, however, died in 1833 without ever having made the breakthrough in refining his slow and inadequate process to allow its useful and practical application. Instead, the glory that could have been his went to another Frenchman, artist, scientist and entrepreneur, Louis Jacques Mandé Daguerre, who used Niépce's hard-won victories as the stepping stones towards the achievement of his own ambition to devise and publish a practicable photographic process.

Daguerre was born in 1789 at Cormeilles-en-Parisis, France. During his childhood in Orléans, he showed artistic talent which eventually led him to the world of the theatre as a scene painter and set designer. A fascination with the creation of visual illusions led to his highly successful career as creator of the 'diorama', an illusionistic picture show involving clever tricks of light for which Daguerre created highly realistic images. Daguerre, and his partner Charles Bouton, followed up the success of their Paris 'diorama' with the establishment of another 'diorama' in London in 1823. As well, the camera obscura became one of the tools of Daguerre's trade and, through the 1820s, he became obsessed with the idea of fixing its fugitive images.

Daguerre first entered into correspondence with Niépce in 1826, and by 1829 had sufficiently impressed him with his knowledge, talents and industry so that he was able to persuade Niépce to enter into a partnership to pool their resources; this despite Daguerre's having so far failed to produce even one transient image.

It was in 1835, after his partner's death, that Daguerre, having built his techniques on the groundwork prepared by Niépce, made the major discovery that was to herald the dawn of photography as a practicable science. This was the discovery of the so-called 'latent' image and was the result of pure chance. Returning to a cupboard where some days previously he had left yet another blank, seemingly fruitless exposed plate, Daguerre was amazed to find a distinct image on the plate. A process of deduction led him to the realization that the 'development' of this image had been effected by the vapours given off by a few drops of mercury spilled from a broken thermometer.

The significance of this discovery was the dramatic reduction in exposure time from hours to half an hour or less. A last hurdle, however, remained: despite Daguerre's premature claims of total success, he had yet to find a satisfactory fixing agent. This he achieved in 1837 with the discovery of the effectiveness of a common salt solution. Daguerre's earliest successful daguerreotype – as he chose to name the products of his process – was [a] still-life composition of plaster casts and other items on a windowsill dating from 1837.

Flushed with his success, Daguerre set about publicizing his discovery, attracting attention as the inventor of the first effective photographic process and hoping to derive financial reward for his momentous

Madame Daguerre *(daguerrotype/ c.1837)* Very few daguerrotypes by the inventor of the process have survived. This example, preserved in London's Science Museum, is a simple, very human portrait by Daguerre of his wife.

Portrait of a mother and her son *(small whole-plate daguerreotype/ c.1850)* Daguerre's invention was used above all for portrait photography. Many practitioners produced mediocre results, and the fine portrait is a rarity. This anonymous example is distinguished by its size and presentation, but above all by its clarity and tenderness.

discoveries to be divided between himself and Niépce's son and successor Isidore. Unsuccessful in attracting bids for his secret processes, Daguerre approached a number of eminent men of science, hoping to enlist their help in persuading the government to sponsor him. In François Arago he found the enthusiastic and vociferous go-between he needed, and, thanks to the haranguing of the well-placed Arago, a bill was soon passed granting pensions to Daguerre and Isidore in acknowledgement of Daguerre's invention.

Daguerre became a national hero and the French felt pride in a government showing such munificence towards its talented progeny. Daguerre's day of glory came on 19 August 1839 when the details of the daguerreotype process were made public by Arago.

The public was gripped with excitement. Chemists and optical instrument makers were besieged by photographers anxious to acquire the materials and equipment needed to make their own daguerreotypes; and the process was published internationally, running into countless editions in numerous languages. London's *Globe* newspaper presented a succinct account of the process in the 23 August 1839 edition: 'We now come to the great discovery: A copper sheet, plated with silver, well cleaned with diluted nitric acid, is exposed to the vapour of iodine, which forms the first coating, which is very thin, as it does not exceed the millionth part of a metre in thickness. There are certain indispensable precautions necessary to render this coating uniform, the chief of which is the using of a rim of metal around the sheet. The sheet thus prepared, is placed in the camera obscura, where it is allowed to remain from eight to ten minutes. It is then taken out, but the most experienced eye can detect no trace of the drawing. The sheet is now exposed to the vapour of mercury, and when it has been heated to a temperature of one hundred and sixty-seven degrees Fahrenheit, the drawings come forth as if by enchantment. The last part of the process is to place the sheet in the hyposulphite of soda, and then to wash it in a large quantity of distilled water'. The result was a pin-sharp direct positive image, the fragile surface of which needed to be protected by sealing it under glass.

Daguerre left it to others to devise faster equipment and to make various minor improvements to his basic process. By the time of his death in 1851 daguerreotype photography was practised throughout the world and was established as the primary process for portrait photography. In the United States it was used almost to the complete exclusion of paper processes.

william henry fox talbot

British/1800–1877

"I know few things in the range of science more surprising than the gradual appearance of the picture on the blank sheet."

William Henry Fox Talbot is justly acknowledged as the father of photography as it is known today. It is to him that photography owes both the idea and the development of the negative/positive system, which allows an unlimited amount of positive images to be printed from a master negative.

Talbot was an exemplary product of a heroic age, the early Victorian era which inspired such tremendous achievements in the spheres of science and industry. Talbot had a visionary mind, a wide-ranging and questing spirit and, although best remembered for his contributions to photography, he is significant in a variety of other fields of learning.

24

Study of leaves
(photogenic drawing/1839) This study of leaves would have been made without a camera by the direct superposition of the leaves onto light-sensitive paper. When exposed to light their image was produced in negative directly on the paper.

Born in 1800, Talbot was 33 years old when he was first inspired with the desire to succeed where others had failed, capturing light's fugitive rays. It was in the summer of 1833, while sketching on the shores of Lake Como and reminded of his inadequacy as a draughtsman — that he was, as he subsequently recorded, '. . . led to reflect on the inimitable beauty of the pictures of Nature's painting which the glass lens of the camera [obscura] throws upon the paper in its focus — fairy pictures, creations of a moment, and destined as rapidly to fade away. It was during these thoughts that the idea occurred to me — how charming it would· be if it were possible to cause these natural images to imprint themselves durably and remain fixed upon the paper! . . . and lest the thought should again escape me . . . I made a careful note of it . . . and also of such experiments as I thought would be most likely to realise it, if it were possible.' Already aware of silver nitrate's sensitivity to light, Talbot resolved 'to make a trial of it in the first instance.'

Talbot's first qualified successes were achieved in the summer of 1835 when he produced a number of miniature negative images of views around his home, Lacock Abbey. One of these, a study of a latticed window at Lacock, is the earliest surviving negative and the second earliest surviving photographic image. The tonal reversal, the lengthy exposures, the relatively poor definition and the unreliability of available

The Pencil of Nature (1844) Talbot's The Pencil of Nature, issued in six parts, was the first commercially published work illustrated with photographic prints. Part I, to which this was the cover, as denoted by the manuscript 'I', contained five calotype prints including views in Paris and Oxford.

known fixing agents were problems which dogged Talbot for several years. It was the realization in January 1839 that Daguerre had apparently triumphed where Talbot had so far found only limited success that prompted a second crucial phase of experimentation and activity.

On 31 January 1839 Talbot read a paper to the Royal Society, 'Some Account of the Art of Photogenic Drawing, or the Process by which Natural Objects may be made to Delineate Themselves without the Aid of the Artist's Pencil.' Talbot's photogenic drawing, however, was limited in its potential applications and despite his disclosure on 21 February of the chemicals used, the process attracted relatively little attention and was eclipsed some months later by the excitement attendant on the disclosure of Daguerre's secret. The revelation of the daguerrotype process, made by François Jean Arago, served only to harden Talbot's resolve. 1839 and 1840 found him experimenting with new equipment, determined to create worthwhile images in the camera rather than by superposition.

The turning point came in September 1840 when Talbot discovered by chance — as Daguerre had before him — that a short-exposure, 'latent' image could be developed by the use of an appropriate chemical agent, in this case gallo-nitrate of silver. Talbot wrote that he knew 'of few things in the range of science more surprising than the gradual appearance of the picture on the blank sheet, especially the first time the experiment is witnessed.' He was on the threshold of realizing a dream which was to lay the foundations for the development of photography.

It was not long before his discoveries were made public in a communication to the Royal Society on 10 June 1841, published under the title The Process of Calotype Photogenic Drawing. Talbot had, meanwhile, protected his interests by securing patent rights to his 'calotype' process earlier in the year. This obliged potential practitioners in England to purchase a licence from Talbot as patentee, although it seems likely that Talbot's motive was probably the desire for full personal acknowledgement rather than for financial reward.

In the first stage of Talbot's calotype process, paper was coated with nitrate of silver and iodide of potassium, to form silver iodide. The iodized paper was then sensitized with solutions of gallic acid and nitrate of silver. The paper was then exposed and the latent image developed with an application of gallo-nitrate of silver sol-

26 ution. An important subsequent discovery and refinement was the efficacy of hyposulphite of soda as a fixing agent. After translation from negative to positive print, the end product, known variously as calotype, Talbotype, or Sun Picture, was a warm-toned image, ranging in colour from greyish- to reddish-brown with a matt surface and a softness in the detail as the inevitable result of having been printed through a paper negative.

Talbot's achievements as a pioneer of photography went beyond these preparatory stages of basic technical innovation. He was to show his sense of vision in the application of photographic processes in book illustration and he effectively discovered the principle of the half-tone screen which would allow the transfer of the photographic image to the printed page. Talbot also proved himself to be a photographer of considerable sensitivity, leaving a substantial body of work which demonstrates, through countless delightful images, a spontaneous sympathy with the aesthetics of a medium in which he had no precursors, and few contemporaries against whom to measure himself. His portraits of family, friends and staff, his studies of surroundings and places visited are imbued with a sense of, life and enthusiasm which is often sadly lacking from the work of so many who were to follow in his footsteps. In Talbot's wife's words, each of his images was 'a little bit of magic realised.'

Bonnets *(calotype/ 1846)* Talbot took a number of photographs of collections of objects lined up on shelves. These included studies of glass, porcelain and silver objects, and this charming and evocative study of the fashionable bonnets of the period. Talbot must have sensed great excitement and reward at having discovered how to make a lasting record of the people, the places and even the most unassuming objects which made up his world.

27

david octavius hill and robert adamson

1802–1870/British/1821–1848

"They (calotypes) look like the imperfect work of man . . . and not the perfect work of God."

(D O Hill)

In the first decade of photography, the vast majority of portraits were daguerreotypes, but it was WILLIAM HENRY FOX TALBOT's invention of the calotype — a paper negative and positive process patented in February 1841 — which led to the earliest masterpieces of portraiture. As *The Quarterly Review* stated in 1857: 'It was in Edinburgh, where the first earnest, professional practice of the art began, and the calotypes of Messrs Hill and Adamson remain to this day the most picturesque specimens of the new discovery.'

Talbot was persuaded not to go to the expense of patenting the calotype in Scotland by Sir David Brewster, a leading Scottish scientist and inventor of the kaleidoscope and lenticular stereoscope. Instead, Brewster recommended that his 21 year old friend Robert Adamson, who suffered from ill health, should become a professional calotypist and Adamson set

28

Revd Mr Moir and John Gibson *(calotype/1843–1848)* Hill's friend John Gibson and his colleague look relaxed, but they are posed with every aid to keeping rigidly still. Moir's right elbow is supported by a book on a table, while his left hand supports his chin. Gibson, braced against the back of a chair, holds a large leather-bound book in his hands. It is exactly the pose in which he appears at the right-hand edge of Hill's mammoth *Disruption Painting*.

James Linton *(calotype/1845)* Newhaven, just outside Edinburgh, was originally a Huguenot village. Hill and Adamson, like many others, were attracted by its picturesque cobbled streets and grey stone houses, its fishing boats and their owners' colourful costumes. The Newhaven pictures, though scarcely 'reportage' or 'photo-journalism' in the modern sense, are an unusually early and complete photographic documentation of a working community.

up his studio at Rock House, Calton Hill, Edinburgh, on 10 May 1843.

David Octavius Hill, 19 years older than Adamson, had already lived in Edinburgh for over 20 years. A landscape painter and lithographer, he was also Secretary to the Royal Scottish Academy of Fine Arts. Eight days after Adamson's arrival in the city, Hill witnessed a major event in Scottish religious history with the mass resignation of 155 ministers from the Church of Scotland, followed five days later by the establishment of a new 'Free' Church by nearly 500 ministers. He determined to paint a mammoth commemoration of the event, similar to the popular paintings of such artists as Benjamin Haydon and Sir George Hayter, whose famous *The Great Reform Bill, 1832* had been put on show in London a few weeks earlier. Most of the participants in the historic ceremony lived outside Edinburgh, and Hill faced the daunting task of sketching them before they left the city. Brewster put him in touch with Adamson, and within days invitations were on their way to the Free Church ministers requesting they sit for their portraits, to be taken as preliminary studies.

Those who accepted the invitation arrived at Rock House only to be shown into the garden. The calotype process was so slow that it necessitated working outdoors while the day was at its brightest between 10am and 2pm. During these hours, the overhead sun cast strong, unflattering shadows onto the sitters' faces which Hill and Adamson softened by reflecting light onto them with a specially-made mirror.

When the partners' photographs were first exhibited at the Royal Scottish Academy in 1844, they were described as being 'Executed by R Adamson under the artistic direction of D O Hill'. This makes it clear that, while Adamson concentrated on technical matters, Hill concerned himself with design, although on at least one occasion the pose was arranged by Sir William Allan, President of the RSA, and other fellow artists may well have tried their hands. The poses reflect Hill's academic training and are in the tradition of Scottish portrait painters such as Sir Henry Raeburn and Sir John Watson-Gordon. Sitters were asked to rest their backs, arms and hands on chairs, tables, huge books or fashionable umbrellas, which helped them to keep motionless during the very long exposures, as did the heavy iron tripod whose over-painted outline can be seen at the top left of the portrait of John Julius Wood as well as in other portraits.

Academic tradition also prompted a dramatic, Rembrandt-like use of lighting.

Even before Adamson's collaboration with Hill, his work was praised for having 'all the force and beauty of the sketches of Rembrandt' and the painter John Harden thought the partnership's portraits comparable with 'Rembrandt's, but improved'. Another painter, Clarkson Stansfield, wrote of his own album of their calotypes that he would 'rather have them than the finest Rembrandt's I ever saw'.

Hill and Adamson did not only take portraits of ministers. They photographed women in the style of fashion plates of the time; children, usually asleep when they kept still; and buildings, especially those in Edinburgh's Greyfriars Churchyard. Their photographs of the colourful fisherfolk of Newhaven, romantically posed in their Sunday best, are among the earliest of working people in their own clothes and

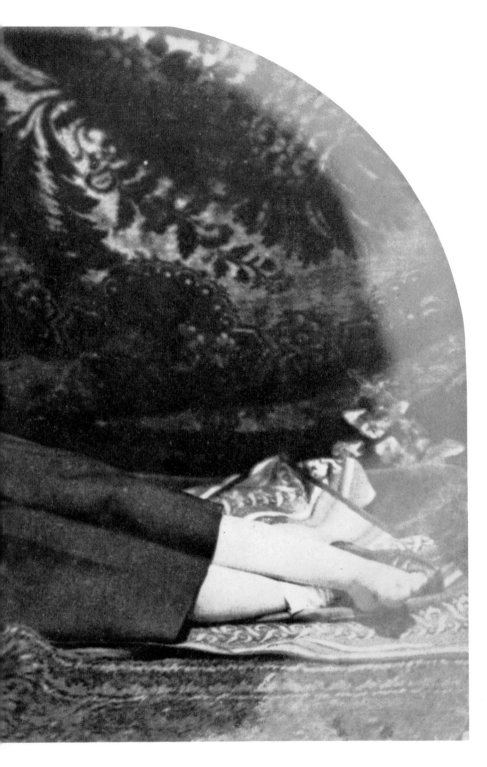

A Sleeping Child 31
(calotype/1843–1848) Elizabeth Logan, daughter of Sheriff H J Logan, of Forfarshire, is photographed asleep because this is one of the few times when a small child can be expected to keep reasonably still! From a first glance at the furniture and heavy brocade in this picture, it appears to have been posed indoors. In fact, as the ivy growing in the corner shows, it was actually taken in the garden of Rock House, Edinburgh.

their own environment.

In December 1847, the sickly Robert Adamson went home to St Andrews hoping that a change of air might improve his worsening health, but on 14 January 1848 he died. In four and a half years, his partnership with D O Hill had produced some 2,500 calotypes, of which Helmut and Alison Gernsheim wrote in their monumental *History of Photography* (1969): 'Today David Octavius Hill and Robert Adamson are universally accorded first place in the annals of photography. The artistic spirit with which their photographs are imbued has impressed all succeeding generations, and it is indeed astonishing that in its very first years the new art should have reached its highest peak in the magnificent achievements of these two Scottish photographers.'

gustave le gray

French/1820–1862

" Photography will play a major role in the development of Art."

Established in France in 1852 by Louis-Napoleon Bonaparte as a result of the 1848 Revolution, the Second Empire was an era of authoritarian rule and economic stability. Universal male suffrage, rapid technological change, and a solid economy were all responsible for propelling France into the modern world. The newly discovered art of photography was the ideal medium for documenting this quickly changing society, and French photographers were responsible for many technological advances in the medium.

Gustave Le Gray was an influential artist who refined and disseminated various photographic chemical processes. Trained as a painter in the studio of Paul Delaroche along with future photographers ROGER FENTON, Charles Nègre, and Henri Le Secq, Le Gray painted landscapes and portraits, exhibiting his work in salons between 1843 and 1861. During the mid-1840s he learned of the work of Alphonse-Louis Poitevin, a photographic chemist who later developed the carbon print, collotype, and refined the photolithograph. By 1848 Le Gray had established himself as a leading figure in the Parisian photographic scene.

In 1839, after seeing his first daguerreotype, Paul Delaroche had proclaimed that 'From today, painting is dead!', thereby provoking a controversy over the aesthetic possibilities of photography which was at its most fierce in the 1850s. Le Gray entered into the fray in 1850 when he submitted nine photographs on paper to a fine arts exhibition in Paris. The jury, as quoted in *La Lumière*, the journal of the Société Héliographique, found 'These works worthy to compete with the most accomplished examples of art', and marvelled at their 'surprising perfection'. It was decided that Le Gray's prints should be shown with lithographs, but the jury was overruled and the photographs dismissed as being products of science rather than art. This debate was re-enacted again and again and climaxed in 1862 when the organizers of the International Exhibition in London decided to show photographs alongside photographic equipment, instead of prints, drawings, or paintings.

Le Gray was as interested in chemistry as aesthetics, and although he published

32

Seascape *(1850s)* 33
Le Gray's seascapes
caused a great
sensation due to his
ability to combine a
detailed sky with
water. He did this
by making prints
with separate
negatives for sky
and sea and he
often made different
combinations of
favoured elements.
The seascapes are
large albumen
prints and the
negatives were
collodion on glass.
By exploiting
dramatic lighting
conditions and
through masterful-
printing, Le Gray
was able to impart
to his natural, often
seen subject, a sense
of monument and
grandeur.

34 **Ship in harbour** *(1855)*
Like many of his
colleagues, Le Gray
turned his camera
on realistic everyday
subjects. However,
his sure control of
the difficult
collodion on glass
process and his
compositional
abilities enabled him
to make images
which satisfy both
documentary and
aesthetic concerns.
In this view of a
ship in harbour, one
of a series made
around 1855, Le
Gray took full
advantage of the
ship's watery
reflections. The
water's stillness
implies a long
exposure.

the results of his experiments with collodion on glass in 1850, he continued to believe in the superiority of paper negatives. His improvement of FOX TALBOT's calotype process was published in 1851. Le Gray's technique consisted of waxing the surface of a sheet of paper and making it light-sensitive. The paper was exposed, creating a latent negative image made visible through development, and then printed onto another sheet of paper to produce a positive image. One drawback to calotypes was that fibres in the paper caused the image to lose sharpness; the additional step of waxing was an important improvement as it made the paper more translucent thereby allowing greater sharpness and detail.

Le Gray was generous with his new technique and before its publication taught the process to Henri Le Secq and C Mestral. He also gave lessons in the waxed paper process to Maxime DuCamp and Charles Nègre, and it soon became the preferred method for photographing architecture and landscapes. Le Gray used the paper negative to great effect in the series of photographs he made during the 1850s in the Forest of Fontainebleau. The forest was a favourite of the Barbizon painters, and Le Gray made compositions of carefully balanced light and dark areas of foliage, the earth, and the sky.

In 1851 the Commission des Monuments Historiques was founded to document important historic architecture in

36 France. Concerned particularly with those buildings whose future was uncertain, the government commissioned five leading photographers to record the sights of various regions. Le Gray and his former student Mestral were assigned to the Aquitaine and the Midi, working there with the waxed paper process.

Le Gray's reputation rests, however, on his seascapes. First exhibited in London in 1856, they were made with collodion plates and printed on albumen paper. By combining two negatives — one of the sky and another of the sea — Le Gray was able to produce prints with fine detail shown in both, something impossible to achieve with one negative. The collodion emulsion was extremely sensitive; ordinarily, skies appeared blank because of the long exposures needed to render a darker ground. Le Gray's large format seascapes are stunning both in their technical and aesthetic achievements.

In 1857 Le Gray was commissioned to photograph the military camp of Chalons.

He recorded scenes of training activities, 37
made a series of officers' portraits, and
photographed Napoleon III's visit. A
founding member of the Société Héliographique and the Société Française de
Photographie, Le Gray exhibited in almost
every major international exhibition.

**Forest of
Fontainebleau**
(1850s)
Le Gray photo-
graphed in the
Forest of
Fontainebleau using
the waxed paper
process which
enabled him to
achieve a delicate
modelling of detail
and tone. His early
training as a painter
undoubtedly enabled
Le Gray to make
clearly seen and
composed pictorial
images such as this.

nadar

Gaspard Félix Tournachon/French/1820–1910

"The portrait I do best is of the person I know best."

Mid-nineteenth-century Paris was, almost as much in fact as in fiction, a city of Bohemians. Poets, painters, writers and musicians starved in garrets, drank in the cafés of the Latin Quarter, flirted with beautiful seamstresses and models, and preached revolution. Their romantic life-style was immortalized in Puccini's opera *La Bohème*, based on the play by Henri Murger, himself a leader of 'la vie Parisi-enne'. In both the opera and the play, the character of the painter Marcel seems to

have been partly based on one of Murger's friends, a man who, although he counted painting among his many talents, earned his greatest success as a photographer. His name was Gaspard Félix Tournachon, but he is remembered by his celebrated pseudonym, Nadar.

From the age of 18, and throughout his life, Nadar was a journalist and writer, and his first novel foreshadowed *La Bohème*. By adding cartoons to his journalistic skills, Nadar planned to publish a series of

38

Gustave Doré *(albumen print/c.1855)* When Nadar joined the *Journal pour Rire* as a contributor in 1849, Doré was already its star cartoonist – at the age of 17. Later, as a photographer, Nadar took several portraits of his colleague and life-long friend, who became France's most celebrated cartoonist and illustrator. Doré's oil paintings were never accepted in his own country, but sold so well in England that he was able to open his own Bond Street gallery.

Gioacchino Rossini *(albumen print/c.1856)* Rossini's luxuriant hair is in fact a wig which he claimed to wear only for the sake of warmth. By the time of this portrait – taken within a year or so of the opening of Nadar's studio – the great Italian composer had given up writing operas for over a quarter of a century. He was content to rest on his laurels, accepting as his right the homage of musicians, the public – and also photographers.

George Sand
(albumen print/ c.1861) The French novelist George Sand was such a celebrated writer that when Nadar published his lithographed *Panthéon Nadar* in 1854 its 300 literary figures were depicted lining up behind a bust of her. Aged 60 and a grandmother when this portrait was taken, she had become Nadar's friend, and a godmother to his son Paul, who was later to take over his father's photographic business.

40

caricatures of one thousand French celebrities, to be entitled *Panthéon Nadar*. Like DAVID OCTAVIUS HILL a decade earlier, Nadar seized on photography as a way of making reference material for his cartoons and persuaded his younger brother Adrien to learn the art and open a studio in the fashionable Boulevard des Capucines.

The first issue of *Panthéon* appeared late in 1854, attracting considerable attention but failing to make a profit. Nadar took up photography himself and opened first a modest studio in the rue St Lazare, and then a grander one a few doors away from his brother's. It is said that Nadar painted this bright red inside and out to match his hair or to reflect his radical politics, but it probably owed more to his flamboyance and flair for self-promotion, also shown in the giant illuminated signature 'NADAR' which dominated the front of the building. The colourful façade attracted an impressive array of sitters including the writers Baudelaire – a particular friend, of whom Nadar wrote a biography – Flaubert, Victor Hugo and George Sand. There were also composers such as Berlioz, Liszt, Rossini and Wagner, and painters such as Corot, Courbet and Manet. These, and many more, were not just sitters, but friends: 'The portrait I do best is, of the person I know best', Nadar wrote.

Nadar's photographic style was neither as original nor as theatrical as his flamboyant personality might suggest; although he used the relatively new wet collodion process, many of his early portraits might have been taken by any one of the daguerreotypists who worked during the 1840s and 1850s. The sitters are usually shown from the waist up, against a plain background, with their hands either out of the picture, in pockets, or tucked inside coats. The portraits are nearly all of men, because Nadar thought photography 'too true to Nature to please the sitters, even the most beautiful'. Exceptions included Sarah Bernhardt.

The most original element of the portraits is the lighting. Initially, Nadar used daylight, arranging his sitters so that the light fell from one side, leaving the body of the sitter unlit, a dark mass above which the face stood out powerfully. Later, he pioneered the use of electric lighting as he was able to delineate features in a more subtle and controlled way, and won the first of several awards for artificially-lit photography in 1861. Although there is no evidence that JULIA MARGARET CAMERON knew Nadar's work, she shared his use of directional lighting and emphasis on faces.

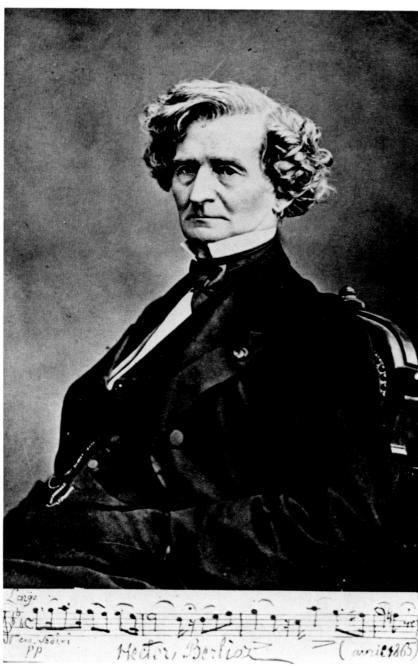

Hector Berlioz
(albumen print/ 1865) Nadar's musical tastes favoured Meyerbeer, Offenbach and Rossini but, when he added a handful of composers to the literary celebrities in *Panthéon Nadar*, Berlioz joined the three more fashionable figures. Aged over 60 at the time of this portrait, Berlioz was enjoying little public success and his mammoth opera on the story of Troy had been a failure. His pose is sad and tired – but not totally defeated.

41

was surrounded by the enemy. Nadar observed the Prussian forces from the air, and, although his political opinions led him to refuse to carry out any attacks on them, he organized regular balloon trips over their lines, carrying mail and telegrams. These included his own letters to *The Times* of London and *L'Independence Belge* of Brussels urging peace, as did the millions of leaflets he scattered from the balloons.

After the war, Nadar, by then a respected public figure, took fewer and fewer photographs. He gave up the grand Boulevard des Capucines studio, although he earned another footnote in art history by letting it to the Impressionist painters for their first exhibition in 1874, and he increasingly left the running of his new, smaller studio to his son Paul. However, father and son made one more pioneering contribution to the development of photography. In 1886, to mark the hundredth birthday of the eminent chemist Michel-Eugène Chevreul, *Le Journal Illustré* published the first ever photo-interview. The questions were asked by Nadar, and the 13 photographs were taken by Paul.

In 1900, Nadar's photographs were shown, along with items illustrating his many other activities, at the Paris Universal Exhibition. He lived through the first decade of the new century, but by then was out of his time. Nadar and the intellectual giants he photographed belonged firmly in the nineteenth century.

She brought her camera even closer to the sitter than Nadar, and her portraits are thus more harshly revealing. While Cameron could not match Nadar's sense of design and smooth professionalism, she would surely have echoed his belief in '. . . the sense of light, an artistic feeling for the effects of varying luminosity and combinations of it'.

Having successfully mastered studio electric lighting, Nadar took his cumbersome equipment into the sewers and catacombs of Paris, and, seeking yet another challenge, he took his first aerial photograph from a balloon in 1858. Ballooning became one of Nadar's obsessions and he financed the building of the huge 'Le Géant', whose inaugural ascent in October 1863 was watched by nearly a quarter of a million spectators. Two weeks later, the balloon went out of control and crash-landed in Germany. Nadar acquired a broken leg and a great deal of publicity, becoming even more of a celebrity.

In 1870, two months after the outbreak of war between France and Prussia, Paris

edouard-denis baldus

German-born French/1820–1882

"Each of these prints is a poem, at times savage, imposing, fantastic . . . at times calm, melancholy, harmonious."
(Ernest Lacan in La Lumière)

Although many of the great early French photographers were painters who turned to the camera later in their careers, an interesting aspect of early French explorations into the medium is the noticeable lack of painterly imitation and effect. The French seemed to sense and seize upon the unique reproductive abilities of the newly developed technology, and realized that photography was the perfect tool by which to document their rapidly changing country. Edouard-Denis Baldus was one of the most successful proponents of the new medium and produced a body of work which provides a rich pictorial record of nineteenth-century France.

Baldus was born in the German province of Westphalia in 1820 and later became a naturalized citizen of France. Between 1840 and 1850 he spent some time in New York, worked as a portrait painter, and showed religious paintings at several Parisian salons. Baldus gave up painting for photography, however, and in 1851 he became a founding member of the Société Héliographique, the first French organization founded to promote photography.

From the start, Baldus showed a special interest in photographing architecture. He quickly mastered the calotype process, and was soon producing prints which rendered the textures of his subjects with great subtlety. In the 1850s the French government became concerned with preserving endangered national monuments and formed the Commission des Monuments Historiques. In 1851, Baldus, along with Hippolyte Bayard, GUSTAVE LE GRAY, Henri Le Secq and C Mestral, were assigned to different parts of France and instructed to photograph buildings and sites of national significance. That year Baldus worked in Fontainebleau, Burgundy, and the Dauphiné; the following year was partly spent in the Midi and Provence, working for the Ministry of the Interior. Baldus' productivity and his superlative ability to photograph architecture was rewarded by more government patronage (it has been suggested that Baldus rarely worked for his own pleasure, more usually on assignment), and he became one of the most successful photographers of the day.

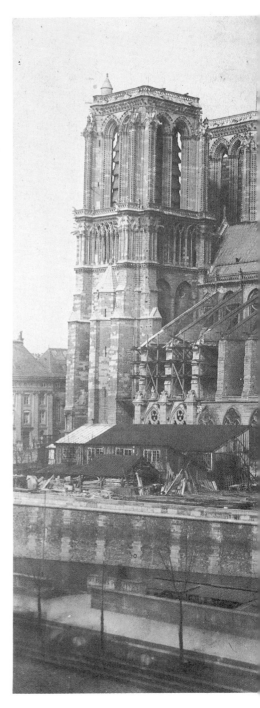

42

Notre Dame   43
(c.1850) Baldus'
interest and skill in
photographing
architecture is
evident in his view
of Notre Dame.
Begun in 1163 and
long the major
religious site of
France, the Cathedral
had slowly fallen
into disrepair until,
in 1841, a 23-year
long restoration
project was begun
by Viollet-le-Duc.
Baldus' photograph
was made during
that period and the
Cathedral is seen
from across the
Seine, soaring
upward from its
foundations.

44

In addition to his work in the provinces, in 1852 Baldus began work on a mammoth project: for the next five years he documented the renovation and expansion of the Louvre. Baldus photographed the façade of the Louvre from every angle, making 1500 photographs of the new wing alone, and these were published in two different series of several volumes.

Baldus' approach to photographing architecture was sophisticated, and differed from that of many of his contemporaries. While others made images which described only the façade, Baldus, by employing odd points of view and perspective, was able to suggest the entire mass of a building. The mystery and arrangement of space in great buildings like Chartres Cathedral and the Louvre are well depicted in Baldus' pictures; his mastery of printing techniques, and the large format he often worked in, add to the impression of space.

During the next few years Baldus travelled throughout France, working on a number of different projects. In 1854 he made a photographic journey through the Auvergne with a former student, Fortune Petit-Groffier; the same year he exhibited 32 photographs of prize-winning animals at an agricultural exhibition in Paris. In 1855 Baron James de Rothschild commissioned Baldus to make a series of photographs along several newly completed railway lines and the resulting industrial views and landscapes, which Baldus composed with great care and

attention to detail, were bound into handsome commemorative volumes, the British Queen Victoria receiving one as a memento of her trip to Paris for the 1855 *Exposition Universelle*. Baldus' panoramas and landscapes were well represented at the Exposition and Ernest Lacan, writing in *La Lumière*, said, 'Each of these prints is a poem, at times savage, imposing, fantastic, . . . at times calm, melancholy, harmonious, like a meditation by Lamartine'. For his work, Baldus was awarded a medal.

Like many of his colleagues, Baldus was interested in the development of new photographic chemistries. He worked with paper and glass negatives, made albumen- and gelatin-coated prints. Indeed, he invented the gelatin technique, and was a proponent of heliogravure. One of the major concerns in photographic circles of the period was the problem of permanence as photographic prints were likely to fade, and the instability of the photograph made its commercial future uncertain. For this reason an alternative to the silver print seemed desirable and photographers began to experiment with photomechanical printing processes, believing that an ink-based technique would provide both permanence and inexpensive mass reproduction. In 1853 Baldus began to make heliogravures and he produced much of his work using this technique.

The contributions of Baldus and his colleagues are particularly valuable in that the cities and countryside they docu-

The Panthéon *(1850s)* This huge church, completed in 1789, served as a necropolis during the reign of Louis-Philippe and as headquarters for the Paris Commune in the 1870s. Many French citizens are buried in its crypt including Voltaire, Zola, Rousseau and Victor Hugo.

Louvre Bibliothèque *(c.1855)* The renovation and expansion of the palace, carried out by Napoleon III, was photographed by Baldus over a period of five years. This view is a good example of Baldus' masterful handling of light and attention to architectural detail.

mented have changed radically since their day. Even as they worked, the old city of Paris, filled with tiny streets and ancient buildings, was being transformed by Baron Haussmann into a modern showplace traversed by broad, straight boulevards. Appointed by Napoleon III in 1853, Haussman's plan for Paris necessitated the demolition of many old buildings and ancient *quartiers*. The photographs made by Baldus, Marville, Bayard, and Nègre, among others, are a vivid documentation of the city that Haussman irrevocably changed. Baldus apparently gave up photography in response to the soaring popularity of the *carte-de-visite*, visiting cards, which carried a photograph of the bearer, which he thought vulgar.

francis frith

British/1822–1898

"His views of Philæ and Luxor are as good as anything Walker Evans did in California a hundred years later." *(Cecil Beaton)*

Francis Frith's first tentative ventures into photography were made in the early 1850s, doubtless as an adjunct to the activities of the printing company which he ran for a few years until 1856. It was not long before Frith was to achieve sudden success as a result of his expeditions to the Middle East between 1857 and 1859. As photography's greatest entrepreneur, he was destined to achieve a lasting reputation and considerable material success, with the development of his publishing company, Francis Frith and Co, founded in 1859, into the largest photographic publisher in the world.

Frith was brought up in a staunch Quaker family, and cherished the ideals to which he was educated. His education was as much practical as formal and he was self-taught in many areas, being of the philosophy that '. . . a man of but one idea or accomplishment is a very sorry distinction, and a still worse foundation for personal happiness.' Frith's life was to be a busy and happy one and surviving accounts would suggest that his family life was as happy as his business activities were successful. His marriage in 1860 to Mary Ann Rosling came shortly after his return from the last of his Middle Eastern journeys and after the foundation of Francis Frith and Co.

The remarkable Middle Eastern episodes were the result of Frith's '. . . quest towards the romantic and perfected past, rather than to the bustling and immature present.' There was a distinctly Byronic flavour to the spirit in which these three journeys were undertaken, and the self-portrait in exotic native dress published by Frith on his return gives the impression that Frith saw himself as a true romantic adventurer.

Frith set sail on his first visit to Egypt in September 1856, travelling up the Nile, seeing and photographing at first hand the spectacular relics of ancient Egypt. Because he was working with the wet collodion process, Frith was obliged to travel with a dark tent, chemicals, bulky and fragile glass plates, and a range of cameras for work in different formats. The negative plates had to be sensitized immediately prior to exposure, and Frith was burdened at every move with cumbersome

46

**Temple of
Komumboo**
*(albumen print/
1858)* This is one of
the 20 exceptionally
large format images
published by Frith
in 1858 under the
title *Egypt, Sinai
and Jerusalem* in a
folio which is
reputedly the largest
photographically
illustrated book ever
published. This
study of a ruined
temple is full of
drama and mystery,
the photographer
making full use of
the almost
theatrical lighting in
a print of exceptional
tonal range and
richness.

47

48 paraphernalia. In an effort to simplify travelling, on one trip Frith took with him a photographic van from England, which was a wicker-work carriage serving as darkroom and sleeping quarters. Not least of these practical difficulties was the problem of working in temperatures so high that on more than one occasion Frith's collodion boiled while he was coating his plates.

Frith returned from his first trip in July 1857 and published a series of 100 stereoscopic views through the firm of Negretti & Zambra, and a series of larger views through Thomas Agnew. These proved to be such an immediate success that Negretti & Zambra were encouraged to sponsor Frith's second trip.

Frith set off in November 1857 on a more wide-ranging tour of the Middle East, taking in the Holy sites of Jerusalem, Bethlehem and Damascus, travelling through Egypt, Sinai, Palestine and Syria, and returning with an extensive selection of negatives in May 1858. These were printed under Frith's supervision and published as stereoscopic views by Negretti & Zambra and in book form with accompanying text by James Virtue. Public response was enthusiastic, and Frith made plans for a third journey, setting off in the summer of 1859 on a journey far up the Nile – a trip remarkable as an exploratory venture, even without the photographic achievement.

Frith's Middle Eastern views were pub- lished in a profusion of bindings and editions and established his reputation as a topographical photographer. Most re- markable of these was the enormous folio volume *Egypt, Sinai and Jerusalem: A Series of Twenty Photographic Views*, the plates being printed from giant 20 × 16in negatives made on his 1858 trip. Thought to be the largest photographically illus- trated book published, this remarkable volume is a memorial to Frith's deter- mination

Throughout the 1860s Frith set about the task of consolidating his Middle East- ern successes with his first trips around Europe and the British Isles, laying the foundation of what was to become the largest topographical picture service in the world. Frith started to document system- atically virtually every corner of Britain, and, as business expanded and demand grew for the Frith Series, he sent pho- tographers all over western Europe and even further afield to add to the already formidable list of available views. The earliest British and European trips were made by Frith himself, and he would travel not only with all his equipment, but

Brighton beach, looking west towards Hove *(albumen print/ c.1890)* One of the many thousands of topographical studies made by the itinerant photographers working for Francis Frith and Co, this image lacks the dramatic lighting, the tonal richness of Frith's own study of Komumboo. It is, nonetheless, a fascinating study of late Victorian life, filled with bustle and activity and crowded with detail.

49

with his entire household as well.

The advent of dry plates in the 1870s greatly facilitated the work of Frith and his staff photographers by reducing the bulk of necessary paraphernalia. However, there is no denying that, with this increased facility, came a decline in the quality of Francis Frith and Co's photographs. As Frith became more involved with running a business rather than taking photographs, the pictures became more predictable, and many of the later Frith Series studies are flat, bland commercial views, of local interest but of little aesthetic merit. The advent of the postcard gave Frith the perfect vehicle for the exploitation of his pictures and, by the time of his death in 1898, there was not a stationer or newsagent in the country that did not stock his postcards.

The story of Francis Frith's evolution from romantic adventurer to prosperous businessman might be read as an analogy of the story of photography itself in its evolution from the magical medium and a handful of spirited pioneers, to the most commercially exploited and subtly pervasive means of visual communication.

roger fenton

British/1819–1869

'Photography a fine art!' exclaimed a well-known painter. 'Why, it is entirely dependent on camera and chemicals.' 'In like manner,' rejoined Fenton, 'as the painter is dependent on pencils, colours and canvas.'

50

York, the west porch *(albumen print/c.1855)* This is a noble example of Fenton's majestic architectural photography. He has filled the frame with the architecture which he is documenting, emphasizing its scale by the judicious inclusion of two human figures. His mastery of technique, as well as his sharp eye, are reflected in his ability to select and translate onto paper a luminous quality of light of considerable tonal subtlety.

Roger Fenton's career in and talent for photography combined the proficiency of a professional with the enthusiasm more readily associated with an amateur. While Fenton earned an income from his photography, the financial rewards were secondary to the satisfaction which he derived from his technical and aesthetic achievements.

Born in Heywood, Lancashire in 1819, Fenton's education included a period at University College, London, commencing in 1838, and a three year sojourn in Paris between 1841 and 1844 where he studied and worked as a painter. Fenton then returned to London to study law and qualified as a solicitor in 1847. It was not until the early 1860s, however, that he devoted himself fully to legal practice, the intervening years being devoted primarily to photography.

Fenton's first encounters with photography were in Paris in 1841 where the artistic circles within which he moved were fascinated by the potentials of this infant art. The influence of certain French painter/photographers Fenton encountered in these early years was to prove very significant in forming the photographer's eye.

On his return to London, Fenton experimented with the calotype process, and in 1847 he became a founding member of a loose-knit group of amateurs known as the Photographic or Calotype Club. Fenton expended much energy in the development of this small group into the more formal exhibition society, founded in the winter of 1852 to 1853, which was known as the Photographic Society. It gained Royal patronage the following year. Fenton's efforts in the formation of the Society constituted an important contribution to the development of photography in Britain, coinciding with the publication and development of new processes which superseded or refined Talbot's calotype process. Mercifully for the history of photography, these were not protected by patents.

Little remains of Fenton's work from the 1840s but, perhaps more than any other British photographer, he exemplified and justified the title given to the 1850s of 'the golden age of photography'. This was the decade in which technique, having been

sufficiently mastered, played a secondary role to aesthetic exploration and picture-making. Also, commerce had not yet had the opportunity to capitalize on the medium and debase its language.

Fenton was a photographer of extraordinary diversity and his *oeuvre* embraces a surprising variety of subject matter. There is as well considerable diversity in the various formats he chose for his work, ranging from the miniature, in the taking of photographs for the stereoscope, to the very large formats which he used for various subjects, but with most notable success in architectural and topographical photography.

The earliest surviving body of Fenton's work is the result of a trip made in 1852 to Russia with his friend the engineer Charles Vignoles. These images, made on waxed paper negatives and printed on salted paper, are more than just fascinating early documents on Russia. They are the first indications of Fenton's exceptional eye for composition, form and tone. The series is strangely haunting by virtue of the sensitivity of the photographer's response to the principles of image-making.

Chronologically, the next distinct categories are Fenton's first commissioned photographs, which comprise a series of photographs taken over a period of nearly eight years from 1854 for the British Museum, and a charming series of family portraits commissioned by Victoria and Albert made in the first half of 1854. By this time Fenton had made the transition from paper to collodion on glass negatives and, although many of the British Museum studies, the Royal portraits, and other work from the early and mid-1850s, were printed on salted paper, Fenton was making the transition to the recently introduced albumenized printing papers.

Late in 1854 Fenton was approached by the publisher Thomas Agnew at the suggestion of the War Office, to undertake a trip to the Crimea to photograph the war and those involved in it. By February 1855 he had set sail on a voyage which was to become the most celebrated phase of his career. Although Fenton could not claim to have taken the first photographs of war, his was the first comprehensive documentation of a campaign. The prac-

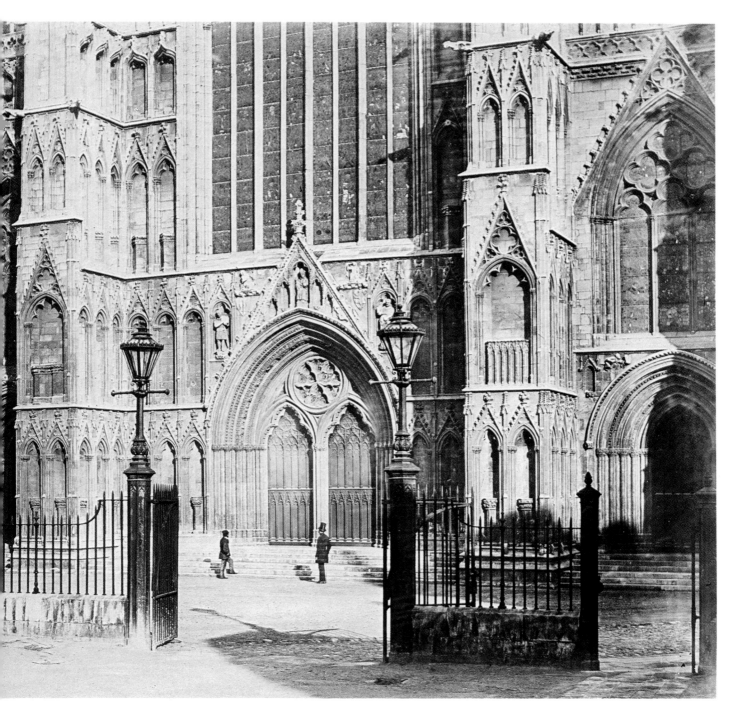

tical problems in undertaking such a journey were considerable and were well detailed by Fenton in an account rendered in January 1856 to the members of the Photographic Society. Most interesting is Fenton's description of the kitting out of his photographic van, a travelling dark-room essential for his work in the field. This vehicle was described by Fenton as '. . . the foundation of all my labours'; and into it were packed his range of cameras, grooved boxes for hundreds of glass plates necessary for such an undertaking, the chemicals and baths required in their preparation and fixing, as well as the books, bedding and other basics needed for such an arduous voyage.

On his return to England, the invaluable experience Fenton had acquired as an itinerant photographer in the Crimea was put to marvellous effect in the resumption of his travels around Britain as a landscape and architectural photographer. The resulting images, made usually in large format and meticulously printed with great concern for tonal subtleties, are the most artistically worthy of Fenton's endeavours. Unlike the still-life studies or costumed *tableaux* which he made at the same time and which, however fine, owe an aesthetic debt to painterly precedents, Fenton's topographical works are distinguished by the purely photographic character of their aesthetic concept. Invariably composed faultlessly, they have strength, dignity, and often romance, and are the understated masterpieces of a sophisticated photographic vision.

In 1862, for reasons unknown, Fenton abandoned photography; the announcement in the autumn of that year of the sale of his photographic equipment clearly demonstrating the finality of his decision. A tempting explanation for this dramatic rupture is Fenton's frustration with the decline in standards — a result of increasing commercial exploitation — of a craft which he had so meticulously practised.

52

Queen Victoria and Prince Albert *(albumen print/11 May 1854)* Fenton was invited, early in his photographic career, to take an extensive series of portraits of Victoria and Albert and their children. This study of the royal couple is distinguished by its naturalness, in marked contrast to the 'stiffness and formality which usually characterize 'official' portraits.

Cook House of the Eighth Hussars *(salt print from collodion on glass negative/1855)* Fenton's objective on his trip to the Crimea was straight documentation, but his instinctive eye for composition made countless memorable images of the subject matter at his disposal. The soldiers are posed in this study as if before a backdrop in a finely balanced painterly tableau.

carleton e.watkins

American/1829–1916

**By his intrepid exploration and imaginative
depiction of the American wilderness,
Watkins led the way for other photographers.**

In the early 1850s, the California Gold Rush drew people from all over the United States to the West Coast. One such newcomer was Carleton Watkins, a young man from northern New York State, whose photographs provide an unsurpassed record of the exploration and exploitation of the American West.

It is difficult to separate fact from fiction in the stories relating the early days of Watkins' career. Like many others, Watkins lost most of his possessions and records in the fire which followed the 1906 San Francisco earthquake. His involvement with photography appears to have been accidental, beginning when he was hired temporarily to replace a daguerreotype operator in the studio of Robert Vance. Knowing that Watkins was totally unfamiliar with the process, Vance suggested that he pretend to make portraits which had already been commissioned. They

54

**Cape Horn,
Columbia River**
(1867) Watkins made this photograph while on a river trip. Seen from the Oregon side of the river, the rock formation rises on the Washington shore. The original print measures 20½ x 16in and is a contact print from a 22 x 18in glass plate negative. The careful diagonal balance of light and dark tones makes a strong graphic image

Cathedral Spires
(c.1865) In search of new subject matter Watkins went on the first of many expeditions to Yosemite Valley in 1861. Using a specially constructed 18 x 22in camera and a wide angle lens which could encompass 75°, he made mammoth views of the region. The appropriately vertical format emphasizes the tremendous height of the trees and rock formations.

55

would be redone at a later date. However, Watkins became interested in learning the process and was soon working in Vance's studio.

Commercially, the daguerreotype was best suited to portraiture. As travel expenses were high and each exposure produced but a single image, it was not until the invention of a reproducible negative that images made outside the studio were marketed on a large scale. Some daguerreotypists, however, did make urban views and landscapes, and it is probable that Watkins would have been familiar with these.

In 1851 the Englishman Frederick Scott Archer invented the wet plate collodion process. This quickly supplanted both the daguerreotype and the calotype, as photographers were now able to make infinitely reproducible negatives. Manual dexterity was a necessity for successful results. Immediately before exposure, a sheet of glass was coated with a wet, light-sensitive emulsion. An exposure of several seconds was made, and the negative had to be developed before the emulsion dried. The wet plate collodion process had its drawbacks; the photographer had to transport an entire darkroom to each location; it was difficult to coat the glass plates evenly; and the fumes given off by chemicals in the dark tent were noxious. Despite all this, the greater sharpness, sensitivity, and reproductive abilities of the wet plate collodion process made it possible for ambitious photographers like Watkins to begin to work with a variety of subjects.

Watkins learned the wet plate collodion technique and, by 1859, was photographing in the Mariposa area west of Yosemite, California. These images were used as the basis for wood engravings which were reproduced in *Hutching's California Magazine*. As more photographers began to work out of doors, competition increased, and Watkins had to travel further afield to make significantly different landscapes. He had an 18 × 22in camera especially built, and in 1861 packed his equipment on to a mule and set off to photograph the scenic wonders of Yosemite. Although Watkins' large format images were impressive, the stereoscopic views made on this trip received more acclaim. The stereoscopic camera produced two slightly different images of the same scene which, when seen through the appropriate viewer, gave the illusion of three-dimensionality. Watkins' use of the stereograph was masterful, and his approach was well suited to the spatial complexities of the Yosemite landscape.

Watkins continued to photograph in Yosemite, both independently and as photographer for government-sponsored sur-

Cape Horn,   57
Washington State
(1867) This is
another of the
photographs which
make up the
Columbia River
Iseries. The man in
the sailing boat was
probably John
Stevenson, a local
resident who acted
as guide for Watkins
while he was on his
trip. The glassy
smoothness of the
water is due to a
long exposure.

vey teams. Public interest in his work was high, and in 1867 he opened the Yosemite Art Gallery in San Francisco. The gallery's name reflected Watkins' main, but not sole, interest. His first and most artistically important trip outside California was also made that year. Watkins left the newly opened gallery, went first to Portland, Oregon, and then journeyed up the Columbia River making panoramas in addition to single and stereoscopic images. The panoramas were composed of three 18 × 22in prints which were joined together to present a continuous view. Most of the landscapes were duplicated by stereographs made from similar vantage points. Besides the landscapes, Watkins photographed mines, bridges, and newly founded towns. The images which resulted from this trip are often considered among Watkins' finest.

Presentation albums of photographs were very popular in Watkins' day and were often commissioned to commemorate the closing of a business deal, record the completion of a railway line or mine, or document a palatial private home. Watkins also assembled his photographs into albums, paying careful attention to design, typography, and the sequence of images. The Columbia River photographs were produced in this format, and the final result weighed over 60lbs.

In 1870 Watkins was asked to take the place of Timothy O'Sullivan as photographer for Clarence King's ascent of Mounts Shasta and Lassen, California. He brought along three times as much equipment as O'Sullivan usually carried, and had to muster all of his considerable skills to reproduce the subtle tones of the snow-covered views. King was pleased with the results and called Watkins the finest photographer he knew.

A better photographer than businessman, by 1874 Watkins' studio had failed and he was forced to turn the business, including many negatives, over to I W Taber, another commercial photographer, who began to publish Watkins' pictures under his own name. Undaunted, Watkins began again by re-photographing the sites of his most successful earlier photographs, and marketing them under the imprint of 'Watkins New Series'. Although financially able to make the best of an unhappy situation, artistically Watkins came to a standstill, repeating past achievements.

The later years of Watkins' career found him less involved with considerations of his art. In order to keep his business solvent he found it necessary to adapt his subjects to the demands of the public. As well as photographing San Francisco sights, Watkins also took on commercial assignments. In the late 1880s he made over 700 pictures of the Bakersfield, California area for a land developer, and privately photographed many ranches.

The fire which followed the earthquake of 1906 destroyed Watkins' home and its contents, including his collection of negatives and prints. His earlier work, which had been taken over by Taber, was also lost. Soon after the fire Watkins and his family moved to a ranch which had been deeded to him by the Central Pacific Railroad. Plagued for the last years of his life by bad health and failing eyesight, Carleton Watkins died in 1916, at the age of 87. By his intrepid exploration and imaginative depiction of the American wilderness, Watkins had led the way for other photographers like EADWEARD MUYBRIDGE

Oregon Iron Company at Oswego *(1867)* Watkins made this image shortly before pig iron was produced here. No doubt he hoped there would be a demand for prints once the company became established. The men with their horse and cart provide a guide to scale and also bring life to Watkins' view of the newly built community.

Multnomah Falls *(1867)* These falls were upriver from Cape Horn. Watkins made mammoth views of them, emphasizing their height by making a vertical photograph. The landscape is reminiscent of the earlier work Watkins did in Yosemite Valley.

lewis carroll

Charles Lutwidge Dodgson/British/1832–1898

" It (photography) is my one recreation and I think it should be done well."

The early months of 1856 were eventful ones for Charles Lutwidge Dodgson, a Fellow of Christ Church, University of Oxford. A few days after his 24th birthday, he acquired the pen name under which he was to publish his famous works of children's literature, 'Lewis Carroll'. Two months later, he met Alice Liddell, who inspired his most famous book, *Alice's Adventures in Wonderland*, and a few days after that he began to take photographs.

Photography had just undergone a major revolution with the original French daguerreotype and English calotype processes being made obsolete by the invention of the wet collodion negative on glass. This became freely available without patent restrictions, and thousands of cheap

60   Anne Lydia Bond: **Beatrice Hatch** *(watercolour copy of a Carroll photograph/1877)* Lewis Carroll's most celebrated photographs are those of young girls. He was happiest when they agreed to pose in exotic costume, or better still, none at all ('sans habilement', as he tactfully described it). He called this study of 'Birdie' Hatch, one of his favourite nude models, 'a gem the equal of which I have not much hope of doing again'.

Alice Liddell as a beggar-child *(albumen print/ c.1858)* Alice first heard the story of *Alice's Adventures Underground* when Carroll and a friend took the three Liddell children rowing. He later wrote it out, dedicated it to her, and published it in 1865. This picture of one of Carroll's favourite child friends, was according to Carroll's nephews and his biographer, Stuart Collingwood, shown to Alfred, Lord Tennyson, who judged it 'the most beautiful photograph he had ever known'

portrait studios opened up for business. In 1855, Carroll had visited one such business in Ripon, near his family home in Yorkshire, and 'Got my likeness photographed by Booth. After three failures, he produced a tolerably good likeness, which half the family pronounce the best possible, and the other half the worst possible.' Soon he returned, having a portrait taken 'to add to Aunt Lucy's collection'. Carroll, like everyone else, had succumbed to the craze for collecting and giving portraits.

The wet collodion process also encouraged many amateurs to take up photography. One such was Carroll's uncle Skeffington, and when Carroll found that another Christ Church Fellow, Reginald Southey, was also keen, he wrote to Skeffington for advice. On 18 March 1856, Carroll bought a camera in London for just £15. It was delivered to Christ Church at the beginning of May, and Lewis Carroll's portrait was probably taken a few days later by Southey, though Carroll describes another in his diary: 'To try the lens, I took a picture of myself for which Ina [Alice Liddell's sister] took off the cap and of course considered it all her own doing!' From then on, Carroll was to devote more time to photography than to any other activity: 'It is my one recreation and I think it should be done well.'

Lewis Carroll pointed his camera at many different open-air subjects: buildings, statues, gardens. He soon began, however, to concentrate on portraits, although these too were mostly taken outdoors to cut down exposure times. His first sitters were his colleagues at Christ Church. Often dressed in academic robes, they stand, or sit, very much on their dignity. Yet Carroll manages to make them appear relaxed, even though the shortest exposure recorded in his diary is 40 seconds. This relaxation, the twinkle in the eye, even the hint of a smile — almost unknown in other photographs of the period — is one of the elements which make Carroll's portraits unique. It helped, of course, that he knew his Christ Church colleagues so well; only a very friendly medical student would have allowed himself to be taken in such cheerful proximity to skeletons and skulls as did Reginald Southey.

When taking photographs the stammer which afflicted Carroll all his life may for once have been a help rather than a hindrance. Most Victorians must have been overwhelmed by the portraitists' array of photographic equipment — huge wooden cameras, long brass lenses, velvet cloths under which the operators dived in order to adjust focus — but Carroll's sitters were perhaps more concerned for the stuttering photographer than for themselves, being too busy sympathizing with him to worry about their own plight.

Carroll consistently lost his stammer in the company of children and thus, naturally, he spent as much time with them as he could, and of course he took their photographs. A few of his young sitters were boys but, finding them 'not an attractive race of beings', he became increasingly interested only in girls. Alongside his diary entries for March 1863, Carroll listed the names of 103 of them he wanted to photograph; proof that he thought of them all as friends, it is in alphabetical order by their first names. Closest of these friends, was Alice Liddell, the dedicatee of *Alice's Adventures in Wonderland*. The original manuscript has Carroll's photograph of Alice at the end, although his drawing of her has recently been discovered underneath. He had always wanted to be a draughtsman and painter and, had he been good enough to satisfy his own high standards, might never have started taking photographs, which he often signed 'From the artist'.

In pursuit of suitable subjects Carroll often transported his camera and cumbersome wet collodion equipment all over the country. On some of these excursions, he photographed eminent Victorians for, like other amateur photographers of the time, he was a 'lion-hunter'. Tennyson, Millais, D G Rossetti, Ellen Terry and even a couple of 'royals' are among those he managed to capture. Yet Carroll continually pursued young girls, especially those who could be persuaded to pose nude or semi-nude. This was not altogether sexual in motivation as many Victorian artists painted children nude, and JULIA MARGARET CAMERON photographed them. But Carroll's diary does reveal that, not surprisingly, there were battles with parents and chaperons and the problem is hinted at in a letter to the mother of Beatrice Hatch, when he decided to have his 1873 photograph of her in the nude painted by a Miss Bond, of Southsea '. . . I am shy of asking her the question, people have such different views, & it *might* be a shock to her feelings if I did do . . .'

That letter was written in 1877, and three years later Carroll suddenly abandoned photography. Some have suggested this was because of a scandal stirred up by his photographing nude girls; others attribute it to his belief that 'All "dry plate" photography is inferior, in artistic effect, to the now abandoned "wet plate"'. It is surely more likely that, as the sale of his books continued to mount, he realized that the hours he was giving to a hobby, for which he had talent, should be devoted to his true calling, writing, for which he had nothing less than genius.

62

Alice Liddell *(albumen print/ 1859)* When Henry George Liddell became Dean of Christ Church, Oxford, in 1855, he moved into the college with his four children: the eldest, Harry, aged eight, Lorina (usually known as Ina) aged five, Alice aged three, and baby Edith, just one year old. It was Alice who became Lewis Carroll's favourite and this is one of the earliest photographs of her.

julia margaret cameron

British/1815–1879

"I hope to be recording faithfully the greatness of the inner as well as the outer man."

According to the official census, there were 11 residents of Dimbola Lodge, Freshwater, Isle of Wight, on Sunday, 7 April 1861. Five were members of the Cameron family; six were servants. Charles Hay Cameron, aged 66, was a landowner and retired barrister. His wife, Julia Margaret, was aged 45. Born in 1815 and raised in India, married at 23 to a rich and highly placed English administrator in that country, she had always been surrounded by servants and had probably never done any kind of physical work, even housework. Yet in her late forties she was to take up — and master — that most difficult, dirty and cumbersome of nineteenth-century hobbies — photography.

Charles Cameron's lands were in Ceylon

64 **La Madonna Riposata (Resting in hope)** *(albumen print/1866)* Mary Ann Hillier, daughter of a Freshwater shoemaker, lived in the Cameron household as a maidservant for 13 years, and was probably photographed by her mistress more often than any other model. This is one of many religious studies in which Mary assumed the role of the Madonna. The child is Percy Keown, youngest son of a Master Gunner at the nearby Coastal Artillery fort.

La Madonna Riposata Resting in hope.

Carlyle like a rough block of Michael Angelo's sculpture *(albumen print/1867)* Mrs Cameron took this photograph of the eminent historian and lecturer at Little Holland House, London, 'to which place I had moved my Camera for the sake of taking the great Carlyle'. Though she also took a profile on the same occasion, the full-face portrait is one of the most powerful portraits ever taken by her — or any other photographer.

(Sri Lanka today) and after his retirement to the Isle of Wight he often returned to them. During one such visit, late in 1863, his daughter (also called Julia) and her husband gave Mrs Cameron a camera to occupy her loneliness. A typically Victorian wooden box-like affair, it had a French 'Jamin' lens, with a focal length of 12in and a fixed aperture of about f.6 or f.7. Such a lens would have made it virtually impossible to get a whole portrait on the 11 × 9in plate sharp, but that did not matter to Julia Margaret Cameron: '. . . when focussing & coming to something which to my eye was very beautiful I stopped there, instead of screwing on the Lens to the more definite focus which all other Photographers insist upon.'

Mrs Cameron worked hard at her new hobby. She had to teach herself to mix chemicals from the jars which stood in her improvised darkroom; to spread the resulting treacle-like 'wet collodion' over a polished glass plate; to put this in a holder and take a photograph while the solution was still damp (when dry, it lost its photosensitivity); to develop and fix the negative with other home-made formulae; and from it, to make a print. None of this was easy for a clumsy Victorian lady of her age and, to the end of her career, Mrs Cameron's negatives were often uneven and carelessly developed. It was two months before she made a passable negative and even this 'I effaced to my consternation by rubbing my hand over the filmy side of the glass . . . when holding it triumphantly to dry'.

At last, on 29 January 1864, Mrs Cameron overcame the pitfalls of the awful process. Her first portrait, of nine-year-old Annie Philpot, still survives, as does a proud covering note: 'Given to her father by me. . . . My first perfect success in the complete Photograph. . . . This Photograph was taken by me at 1 pm Friday Jan. 29th. Printed – Toned – fixed and framed and given as it now is by 8 pm this same day.' In those seven hours, Mrs Cameron had started her climb to becoming one of the greatest portraitists of the nineteenth century.

However hard and successfully Mrs Cameron worked, she would never have achieved fame had it not been for the fact that her friend and neighbour in Freshwater was Queen Victoria's Poet Laureate, Lord Tennyson. Tennyson soon submitted himself to Julia Margaret's camera and persuaded other celebrities to do the same. It was an ordeal. Professional portraitists were reducing the size of their plates and increasing the amount of light on their sitters in order to cut down exposure times. The *carte de visite* was the universal 1860s portrait, tiny (about 4 × 2¼in),

often full-length and usually devoid of originality or character. Mrs Cameron's 11 × 9in photographs (later increased to 15 × 12in) were 'close-ups', like those of the amateur photographer, David Wilkie Wynfield, who gave her her only lesson. She lit them from one side only (some of her profiles of Julia Jackson used only firelight), and she reckoned her exposure times in minutes rather than seconds. There is scarcely one of her pictures in which some sign of movement cannot be detected.

When Mrs Cameron was photographing Tennyson and his eminent friends, she hoped to be 'recording faithfully the greatness of the inner as well as the features of the outer man'. It was this, perhaps, which led her to take so many profiles. The Victorian 'science' of phrenology was at the peak of its popularity and she possibly felt that, by delineating the exact shape of the heads of writers, painters and scientists, she might distil the essence of their intellectual gifts. It was also presumably easier for them not to have to gaze at a great brass lens during the outrageously long exposures she demanded. Thomas Carlyle, however, outstared her camera triumphantly and *Carlyle like a rough block of Michael Angelo's* [sic] *sculpture* (1867) gains great strength and presence from his visible, almost tangible, willpower.

If it was intellect that drew Mrs Cameron to famous males, it was beauty which dictated her choice of female models. A favourite was her maid Mary Hillier, so often photographed as the Virgin Mary that she was sometimes called 'Mary Madonna'. These attempts to emulate religious painters of the Renaissance may today seem mawkish and ill-judged, but the serene features of Mary Hillier and the deep folds of her head-dress sometimes combine with surprising success. Mrs Cameron also tried to rival painting in a series of illustrations for Tennyson's *Idylls of the King*. Accuracy of costumes and backgrounds obviously interested her no more than sharp focus or fastidious processing, but she cast the characters with great care. The truly regal *King Arthur* (1874), for instance, is one of the porters at Yarmouth Pier.

In 1875, the Camerons went to live permanently in Ceylon. Though Mrs Cameron took some photographs, mainly of Tamil workers on her husband's plantations, her time was mostly taken up with her family. Nursing her son Hardinge when he became ill, she herself caught a chill and died in 1879. An obituary in *The Times* recalled her outstanding portraits of Lord Tennyson, Sir John Herschel and Joseph Joachim, among others, describing them as 'the most picture-like photographs ...which have been given to the world.'

David Wilkie Wynfield (1837–1887): **Frederick Walker as 'a young Florentine nobleman'** *(albumen print/ c.1862)* Soon after Julia Margaret Cameron took up photography, she wrote: 'I have had one lesson from the great Amateur Photographer Mr Wynfield and I consult him (in correspondence) whenever I am in a difficulty'. Wynfield was principally a painter who briefly espoused photography in the early 1860s. To him, Mrs Cameron later wrote: 'I owed *all* my attempts and indeed consequently all my success'.

My niece Julia Jackson, now Mrs Herbert Duckworth *(albumen print/ 1867)* Julia Jackson, the third daughter of Mrs Cameron's younger sister Maria, seems to have been her favourite niece. She married twice and one of the children of her first marriage was Gerald Duckworth, founder of the publishers which bear his name. Two of her children by her second husband were the Bloomsbury figures Vanessa Bell and Virginia Woolf.

eadweard muybridge

British/1830–1904

"The dry plate's most spectacular early use was by Eadweard Muybridge."
(LIFE magazine)

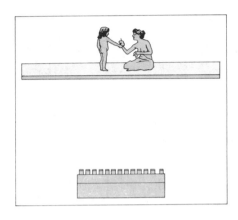

Muybridge took these pictures with a special camera which had 12 picture-taking lenses. Each lens made a separate image on a glass plate so that Muybridge could photograph 12 different stages of one sequence with just one camera.

Child bringing a bouquet to a woman *(photogravure/1885)* Despite difficulties in persuading non-professionals to pose fully or partly nude, Muybridge preferred not to photograph artists' models, who were 'as a rule, ignorant and not well bred . . . their movements are not graceful'. The woman and child here — and in several other *Animal Locomotion* sequences — are the wife and daughter of J Liberty Tadd, Principal of the Philadelphia School of Industrial Art.

Eadweard Muybridge was one of the first men of the nineteenth century to make satisfactory photographic analyses of motion, and the first to find a means of projecting his results. Born in 1830 in Kingston-upon-Thames, England, as Edward James Muggeridge, he emigrated to the United States in the early 1850s, settling in San Francisco and changing his name to sound more 'Anglo-Saxon'. A near-fatal stagecoach accident in 1860 made Muybridge convalescent for several months, and it was during this time that he seems to have taken up photography, soon becoming one of the most successful topographical photographers in the western United States. Muybridge published his first major portfolio, *Scenery of the Yosemite Valley*, in 1867 and the success of this work brought invitations to accompany a military expedition to Alaska to take stereoscopic photographs of lighthouses along the Pacific Coast.

In 1872, Leland Stanford, governor of California and millionaire builder of the transcontinental railroad, asked Muybridge to photograph his world-record trotting horse, 'Occident'. Stanford wanted to prove that at full gallop the horse took all four feet off the ground at one moment. Although it is often asserted that this was to help Stanford win a US$5000 bet, it seems more likely that he simply wanted scientific, factual proof of what he observed with his own eyes. Whatever Stanford's motive, Muybridge achieved his first successes in 1872 and 1873. These first photographs were too blurred to publish, but clear enough to prove Stanford right. There followed a four year hiatus, during which time Muybridge was tried for murdering his wife's lover and acquitted, was sued for divorce and then widowed. He travelled and photographed widely in Central America, going back to San Francisco and the photography of motion in 1877.

Returning to his work with Stanford, Muybridge used a white background for the first time which brought exposure times down to a claimed two-thousandth of a second, taking a photograph of 'Occident' at full stretch. Although still far from clear, the photograph was published in a version so extensively re-touched that it

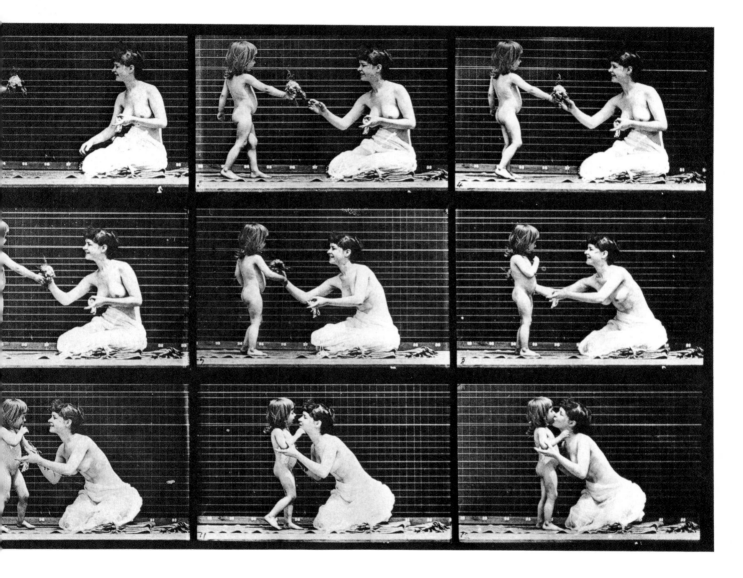

70 became virtually a painting, and it can be seen in the Stanford Museum of Art, California. Because of this extensive re-touching, however, the photograph failed to convince many who saw it.

Nevertheless, Muybridge's experiments continued. Working at Stanford's stud farm, at Stanford's expense and with the assistance of his technicians, Muybridge developed a system of 12 cameras mounted in a line along a rubber track and triggered by 12 trip wires. In June 1878, he showed the press the equipment in use. Six photographs of each of the two horses in the demonstration were published, and this time – although there was still some re-touching – even the sceptics believed. By 1879 the number of cameras in the line had doubled, with five more taking photographs from diagonal viewpoints of horses, dogs, pigs, pigeons, goats and human beings, and in May 1881 Muybridge published *The Attitudes of Animals in Motion, A Series of Photographs Illustrating the Consecutive Positions Assumed by Animals in Performing Various Movements.*

Muybridge proceeded to develop a way to reconstitute the movements of his subjects which he had previously succeeded in freezing; his 'zoöpraxiscope' projected sequences of photographs mounted round the edge of a glass disc to give the illusion of motion. It was the world's earliest cinema projector and the most sophisticated device of its kind until the invention of Thomas Edison's 'kinetoscope' 12 years later in 1891.

During 1881 and 1882, Muybridge set off on a grand European tour, lecturing first in Paris and then in London, where his audiences included the Prince of Wales, Gladstone, Tennyson, Professors Huxley and Tyndall, Frederick Leighton, and many others. On his return to the United States in 1882, he began the difficult task of trying to find US$20,000 for a project to study animal motion and publish 'a Standard Work of Reference for the Painter, the Sculptor, the Anatomist and the Physi-

ologist'. The University of Pennsylvania, Philadelphia, finally offered sponsorship, partly because of its long tradition of scientific enquiry, and perhaps partly because the foremost American realist painter of the time, Thomas Eakins, was professor of drawing and painting at Pennsylvania Academy of Fine Arts and himself eager to photograph the human figure in motion. Under the guidance of an academic committee, Muybridge spent two years photographing almost 2,000 models – male and female, clothed and nude,

Male nude *(photogravure/ 1885)* In his prospectus for *Animal Locomotion*, Muybridge described Model No 95 who is seen in this study as 'an ex-athlete, aged about sixty'. In fact, 'Model No 95' was Muybridge himself, and he was aged 55.

In this plate, one of five in which he appears, he is shown ascending an incline (top); ascending an incline with a 50lb dumb-bell (second row); descending an incline (third row); descending an incline with a dumb-bell (bottom).

71

healthy and handicapped — as well as wild and domestic animals. Some 20,000 photographs of 781 subjects were in *Animal Locomotion*, published in 1887.

Once again, Muybridge set out on a promotional tour in Europe and the United States, to raise subscriptions to *Animal Locomotion*, at US$100 each, but there were not enough buyers. In desperation, he set up his 'Zoöpraxographical Hall' on the Midway at the 1893 Chicago World's Columbian Exhibition but, surrounded by less serious entertainments, it was not well

attended, and failed to increase the list of subscribers. The 'Hall' however was the first cinema ever built, and included the first commercial motion picture shows, anticipating the Lumière Brothers' successful 'Cinematographe' presentations in Paris by more than three years.

At the age of 63, Muybridge was tired, the after-effects of the stagecoach accident many years earlier ageing him prematurely. He thus returned to Kingston-upon-Thames, bequeathing all his photographic equipment to the local library.

Muybridge brought out popular editions of *Animals in Motion* in 1899 and *The Human Figure in Motion* in 1901. Three years later he died, too soon to know that these volumes were to be reprinted frequently and that, nearly a century after their first appearance, the photographs on which they were based were the most complete records of animal motion ever produced. In 1979, the first unabridged selection was re-published and Muybridge's historic contributions to science and art are now seen to be unrivalled.

alfred stieglitz
American/1864-1946

"The ability to make a truly artistic photograph is not acquired off-hand, but is the result of an artistic instinct coupled with years of labour."

It was Alfred Stieglitz's relentless efforts which helped early twentieth-century photographers move away from the prevailing style of imitating painterly effects and subject matter to a more modern, more specifically photographic approach.

Throughout his lifetime, Stieglitz fought for artistic and personal freedom of expression. In publications like *Camera Work* and in New York galleries, he championed avant-garde artists like Picasso, Cézanne, Matisse, and O'Keefe, who were showing their work, often for the first time, to a generally hostile public. In addition to his

energetic defence of all that was new and progressive in painting and sculpture, and despite devoting most of his time to the creation of opportunities for others, Stieglitz was able to produce a body of work which includes many memorable and influential images.

Alfred Stieglitz was born in New Jersey in 1864 to German parents. His father was an unconventional, well-to-do amateur painter and lover of the arts, and Stieglitz was brought up in a liberal atmosphere. In 1881 Stieglitz went to Germany to study mechanical engineering but, two years

72

The Steerage
(1911) Stieglitz made this image while on a transatlantic voyage. Venturing below deck he was moved by the scene which met his eyes and which contrasted so painfully with his luxury first class quarters. This is perhaps Stieglitz's best known photograph and it satisfied both his aesthetic and emotional needs.

Georgia O'Keefe
(1923) Six years after he met her at '291', Stieglitz made a series of portraits of Georgia O'Keefe. In them she plays many roles, constantly changing expression and mood. This harsh close-up conveys the stress in her personality.

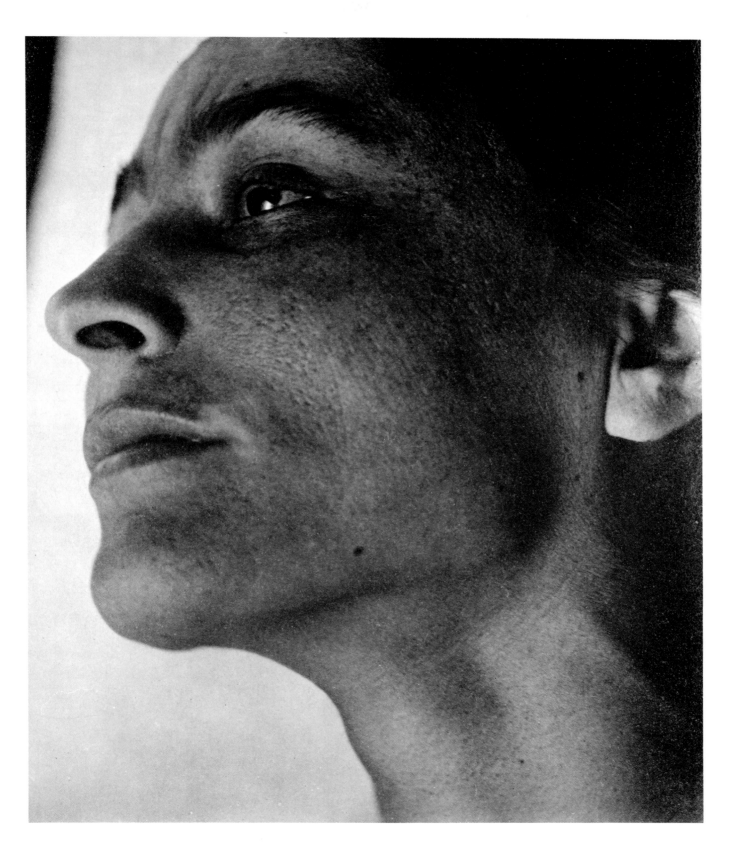

STIEGLITZ

later, he became involved in photography and soon gave up engineering permanently. Photography quickly became an obsession and Stieglitz was determined to master not only the craft but the art. In 1887 he was awarded first prize in an exhibition judged by the prominent photographer PETER HENRY EMERSON. Like most of his contemporaries at this time, Stieglitz was making anecdotal pictures; photographs which told a story and relied heavily on popular genre paintings. His work was so realistic that in 1896, when one of his pictures was published in *The Photographic Times*, many readers thought it was a reproduction of a painting.

Stieglitz returned to New York in 1890 and after an unsuccessful foray into the photoengraving business, began to devote most of his time to thinking about, and making, photographs. Rather than indulge in the vogue for heavy manipulation of negative and print to achieve mysterious and romantic effects, Stieglitz began to pursue a more straightforward approach. He believed that creative expression through photography was best achieved by being true to the special characteristics and reproductive abilities of the camera itself. Although he was able to appreciate and publish the work of pictorialists such as STEICHEN, Kasebier, and White, Stieglitz favoured 'straight' photography until the end of his life.

In order to share his ideas and promote worthwhile work, Stieglitz founded and began to edit *Camera Notes* in 1897, the journal of the Camera Club of New York. He used his position within the club to arrange monthly exhibitions of work which interested him, assembled shows of American photography for salons abroad, and generally championed progressive work. In 1902 conservative elements forced Stieglitz to leave the club, and in rebellion, he founded the Photo-Secession group. This was a group of leading photographers who were, in Stieglitz's words,

'seceding from the accepted idea of what constitutes a photograph.'

Under the direction of Stieglitz, and with the help of Edward Steichen, the Photo-Secession quickly became the dominant school of American photographic thought. As an extension of the movement, Stieglitz began to publish *Camera Work* in 1903, a lavish photographic quarterly. *Camera Work* differed from other photographic journals in that it was intended as a forum for ideas, rather than a technological guide. Portfolios of photographs appeared in each issue, as did criticism, caricatures of prominent photocelebrities, discourses on aesthetic theories, and news from abroad.

In 1908, at Steichen's urging, *Camera Work* broadened its coverage to include work in other media, and drawings and paintings by progressive European and American artists began to appear. Also at Steichen's instigation, Stieglitz opened the first of several galleries in 1905. The gallery '291' served as a catalyst, meeting place, and centre for avant-garde art and artists. Through '291' Stieglitz was able to influence the course of new ideas about art, and provide artists with a much needed supportive and sympathetic environment. Although '291' showed much European work, Stieglitz had a special interest in American art and sought out and exhibited work by John Marin, Marsden Hartley, and Georgia O'Keefe, among others.

Stieglitz eventually wearied of the strains and pressures inherent in publishing and gallery work, and became increasingly convinced that most contemporary photographers lacked vision and moral conviction. However, the appearance of PAUL STRAND, a young photographer who embodied Stieglitz's ideas about a direct, committed photographic vision, gave Stieglitz a new incentive, and the last two issues of *Camera Work* were devoted to Strand's work. Both the maga-

zine and '291' ceased in 1917, and from that time until 1937, when he could no longer handle his unwieldy cameras, Stieglitz increasingly pursued his own work.

Stieglitz's photographs ran from early pictures of New York which depicted scenes of everyday life, to an extended portrait of his wife, Georgia O'Keefe, which comprised hundreds of images, to what he called his 'Equivalents'. The latter were images which Stieglitz felt most closely reproduced inner states of emotion, and were usually pictures of sky, clouds and trees. Stieglitz said of these 'All of my photographs are equivalents of my basic philosophy of life. All art is but a picture of certain relationships; an equivalent of the artist's most profound experience of life.'

Although many of the early New York pictures seem to be indistinguishable from traditional soft-focus pictorialism, Stieglitz rarely tampered with either negative or print. Undaunted by the elements, Stieglitz would often photograph in the rain or snow, sometimes in the middle of the night. Prolonged exposures and hazardous weather often gave his work qualities which others achieved only through artificial manipulation.

The O'Keefe portraits, begun in 1917, are a landmark in the history of photographic portraiture. Stieglitz depicted every aspect of physiognomy, every nuance of emotion and expression, in order to give a total portrait of a complex and sophisticated human being. The themes which run consistently throughout Stieglitz's photographs are a concern with humanity, life, and freedom of expression. He had the ability to combine these ideas with an interest in form, pictorial structure, and an unerring talent for composition. Stieglitz's impact as paternalistic advisor to several generations of photographers was strong. He helped broaden the scope for visual achievement in the twentieth century, and established photography's legitimate claim as a fully expressive art form.

Equivalent *(1925)*
For many years, Stieglitz worked on a series of 'Equivalents'. These were images which he felt represented his most deeply felt emotions. Of all the arts he considered they were most closely related to music. This image of clouds and sky is typical of the group.

peter henry emerson

British/1856-1936

"The modern school of painting and photography are at one; their aims are similar, their principles are rational, and they link one to the other."

Pedro Enrique Emerson was born in Cuba in 1856 on his father's sugar plantation. In 1869 he moved from Wilmington, Delaware, where he had been at school since the age of eight, to his mother's native England. He enjoyed a brilliant academic record as a medical student at King's College, London, qualifying in 1879, and studied further at Clare College, Cambridge, before returning to King's College Hospital as Assistant House Physician, a post won by competitive examination. Peter Henry Emerson, as he now called himself, had already climbed the bottom rungs of a promising medical career when he acquired his first camera in 1882, with the intention of illustrating an ornithological treatise being prepared by a friend.

Emerson brought to photography an extraordinary personal energy which characterized all his endeavours — this was a man who managed to write an autobiographical novel, *Paul Ray at the Hospital: a Picture of Medical School Life*, in the course of his honeymoon and who excelled, according to his own testimony, in some half-dozen sports. Like a comet moving across the rather dull sky of late Victorian photography, the power of Emerson's vision — expressed in images, words and deeds — had by 1886 transformed the aesthetics of photographic picture-making. As an energetic proponent of his views on photography, Emerson lectured, wrote theory and criticism, organized and judged exhibitions, and, most importantly, exhibited and published his own revolutionary photographic images.

Emerson scorned the work of the fashionable English photographer Henry Peach Robinson, criticizing not only the artificiality of the poses used and his spurious sentimentality, but also Robinson's combination printing from multiple negatives, a technique central to Robinson's approach. Emerson was in fact critical of all handwork, even re-touching, believing in the purity of the unmanipulated print and 'straight' photographic vision. Emerson's own credo, which originated largely from an idiosyncratic and hurried understanding of the history and nature of art, was presented in *Naturalistic Photography*, his major theoretical work

76

Gunner working up to fowl
(platinotype/1886)
This picture appeared in the book *Life and Landscape on the Norfolk Broads*. Its co-author T F Goodall introduced the gunner as working his way up to a flock of birds on the Broad 'in the grey morning light which the tone of the plate so well renders.'

first published in 1889. Emerson was influenced by recent theories of colour and developments in French painting especially the work of Courbet, Millet and the Impressionists. For Emerson, 'true art' involved a sensitive, accurate response to natural incident. Painting might be unsurpassed for its chromatic potential, but photography, so absolute in 'line' and faithful to tonal relationships, was, for Emerson, the unequalled medium of artistic expression.

From his great burst of activity in 1885 and 1886, Emerson chose the pictures for his first four photographically illustrated publications: *Life and Landscape on the Norfolk Broads* (1886), *Pictures from Life in Field and Fen* (1887), *Idylls of the Norfolk Broads* (1894) and *Pictures of East Anglian Life* (1888). Although the common theme was the work and environment of the East Anglian peasantry — and for this he must be considered one of the finest early documentary photographers — subject matter was always subordinate to style, and a number of distinct artistic attitudes make their presence felt.

Typical of much of Emerson's early work, an image like *The Grafter* has a specific sociological content, but the picture is even more fundamentally involved with its own aesthetics, showing an indebtedness to Millet in the patterning of light and shadow, added to an inventiveness of composition. In the abstract, undeniably modern image of *Gunner Working up to Fowl*, subject matter disappears, the image presents a dynamic form moving through an atmospheric space in a world generated solely from a narrow range of dark grey tones. The 'dark picture', later invented by Emerson, became a key element of the Photo-Secessionist style, though Emerson was critical of the pigment printing techniques the Photo-Secessionists used to achieve that end.

At the transitional point of his artistic development, in *Wild Life on a Tidal Water* (1890), Emerson turned to the city of Great Yarmouth, Norfolk, as his subject. Some of these pictures show urban men working, but their lasting significance lies in their modernity and abstraction, springing from Emerson's radical decision to use his technique of differential focusing — whereby only one plane in the field of

A Winter's Sunrise *(photo-etching/ 1895)* At the outset Emerson explained Norfolk life. By 1895 he simply reproduced snatches of tales and descriptions of the changing seasons without seeking to instruct or inform. His implication is that things happen indifferently and that man has no option but to accept life as it comes.

78

vision is in sharp focus – for an interior shot; thus 'throwing away' the bottom third of the picture.

Disappointed with previous results but delighted with the fine gravure quality produced by the Coll Brothers for *Wild Life on a Tidal Water*, Emerson gleaned from them the secrets of their craft and in *On English Lagoons* and *Marsh Leaves*, the statement of his final vision, he hand-pulled the gravures himself. In his attitude towards gravure as a 'high art' medium, Emerson was a forerunner of ALFRED STIEGLITZ.

Two years after publishing *Naturalistic Photography*, in 1890 Emerson recanted his views in a pamphlet entitled *The Death of Naturalistic Photography*. The implications of certain experiments taking place concerning sensitometry – the precursor to the light meter – led Emerson to the curious conclusion that photography, being a purely mechanical process, could not aspire to the status of art, the point being that the photographer could not alter tonal values by an act of aesthetic will. Emerson's last year as an active photographer was 1891, in which he produced the images for *Marsh Leaves*, published in 1895. Even in his finest and final work, Emerson incorporated outside artistic influences: *A Winter's Sunrise* bears a resemblance to works of the British landscape artist Samuel Palmer (1805–1881), while *A Snow Garden* resembles an oriental ink drawing.

Snow Garden
(photo-etching/ 1895) Emerson printed 16 images in *Marsh Leaves* in which he describes the return of spring. Occasionally his eye would settle on 'some marsh farm, seen behind a decorative fringe of reed tassel, palpitating in its blue envelope of transfiguring mist'. In 1895 Emerson, increasingly fatalistic, found consolation in such incidental beauties as these.

79

In a Sail Loft
(photogravure/ 1890) Before he took this picture Emerson said he was working with 'a quick exposure on a swift tideway.' It was published in *Wild Life on a Tidal Water.*

eugène atget
French/1856–1927

"His equipment was the most rudimentary – a set of rectilinear lenses and a wooden tripod."
(Cecil Beaton)

Someone once said that Eugène Atget photographed the deserted streets of Paris like a crime photographer gathering his evidence. The old lie which says that the camera never lies might well have been inspired by Atget. His pictures seem to deal exclusively in facts, never in photographic fancies. Atget himself called his photographs 'documents'. When negotiating their sale to the French Archives he rarely charged more than 10 francs a print. An old friend later observed that 'Atget did not know that he was Atget.'

Yet it is ALFRED STIEGLITZ and Eugène Atget who are most frequently called the fathers of documentary photography. From his apartment-cum-studio at 17 bis rue Campagne Première, Montparnasse, Atget collected the details of a disappearing Paris, its streets, streetwalkers, and the alleyways they stood in; its shopwindows and balconies; its plain middle-class interiors and luxurious gardens; its '. . . fine façades and doors, panellings, door knockers, old fountains, period stairs . . .'. Remembering perhaps his 10 failed years as an actor, he might almost have been collecting props for a play about the belle epoque. A typical Atget interior looks and feels like a stage set. All that is missing is the actors and the soft-focus which was all the rage at the time. This lack of pictorial rhetoric, the lack of elaborate compositional devices, dramatic lighting or theatrical perspectives, made his photographs seem like perfect archive material. It also, as William Adams pointed out, 'postponed the recognition of his genius.' But at least it ensured the preservation of most of his output. After his death it was the American photographer Berenice Abbott who rescued the 10,000 carefully numbered and classified negatives which constitute his life's work. At the time few people could understand why anyone had bothered to photograph Paris so often, so purposefully.

Atget was 42 when he decided to leave the theatre and become a photographer. During his own lifetime photography had developed from the single-copy daguerreotype to the multiple print. But Atget was a traditionalist who preferred the old methods to the new. Years later when his friend MAN RAY suggested that he try some

Interior *(c.1905)*   81
Atget's interest in
reflections
encouraged him to
seek out fountains,
ponds and canals,
shopwindows and
mirrors. In his
shopwindows the
reflections from the
street were confused
with the real objects
behind the glass. In
this ornate interior
the mirror creates
uncertainty about
what is real and
what is reflected.
But it is the row of
covered chairs
which are the focus
of the room. They
introduce the gentle
air of surrealism
which often disturbs
the apparent
'ordinariness' of an
Atget photograph.

Le Petit Trianon, Temple d'Amour *(c.1900)* The gardens in and around Paris were Eugène Atget's outdoor studio. It was here that he developed his formal skills. This view of the Temple d'Amour in the *jardin anglais* that Marie Antoinette created for herself at Versailles, is as strikingly simple as the temple itself. Atget's sensitivity to architecture extended not just to his viewpoint but also to the light in which he chose to photograph a building, in this case a bright, crisp winter light which suits the temple perfectly.

82

of the new, more permanent materials, Atget refused. His photographs, he said again, were 'only documents', which would sell just as well using old-fashioned techniques and materials.

Thus Atget continued to use his cumbersome wooden bellows camera with its rectilinear lenses and the wooden tripod to which it was permanently attached. He continued to carry a dozen heavy glass plates around with him in a plate-holder; he made contact prints from the glass negatives and perfected his large, clear images; he took great care over his borders and never cropped them (the same cannot be said of subsequent publishers of his pictures).

Nowadays, the gelatin silver bromide images have faded to a nostalgic brown. Sometimes publishers deliberately publish them in sepia so that they seem, like his subject-matter, to have suffered what FOX TALBOT called 'the injuries of time.' It is only when you see new prints made from the original negatives that Atget's crispness, his cool, grey lighting, is revealed.

Even without their brown haze, Atget's photographs do indeed seem to hark back to the beginnings of photography. Every picture seems to be making a discovery as if the city had never been seen this way before. The photographer's personality guides the viewer through the subject matter but never intrudes upon it.' It is as if reality has been unveiled for the first time and the photographer has merely stood back in admiration. With their fixed

dimensions — all his prints were 7.2 × 9.2in — and fixed viewpoint (the rectilinear lenses were immovable against the image plane), Atget's photographs give the appearance of being a systematic record of the truth.

It was not only urban historians who collected Atget's photographs. The handmade sign above his door read 'Documents pour Artistes' and it was as a supplier of images as material for artists that Atget made most of his living. He had once wanted to be a painter and upon moving to Montparnasse he soon met Vlaminck, Utrillo and Braque.

Man Ray later became a close friend He, Segonzac and Derain certainly used Atget's photographs in their work. Others like Duchamp and Picasso were at least familiar with them. Atget would occasionally help the Surrealists by incongruously superimposing images for them. But a photograph like *Uniforms* does not require any trickery from the photographer to achieve its air of surrealism. The disembodied clothes preserved behind glass are exactly as Atget found them. With their multiple reflections and strange contents, Atget's shopwindows are as eerie as anything the Surrealists could manufacture. In 1926, when he was 70 years old, two of his photographs were reproduced in *La Revolution Surrealiste*, the official Surrealist organ.

Although Atget undoubtedly contributed to the work of his painter friends, it is not easy to see where the painters in-

fluenced him. While most of his contemporaries were using painterly special effects, producing dream portraits and exotic set-pieces, Atget dealt only in reality. A very self-sufficient and single-minded photographer, he heeded little advice and gave even less. During the long apprenticeship which he undertook on his own, he used the suburbs and outlying gardens of Paris for target practice — his early shots of the Tuileries seem to meander all over the paper; some of his statues have been accidently decapitated.

Gradually Atget evolved the directness for which he became famous. The heavy camera, the intractable lenses, provided a steady foundation upon which to work. An Atget photograph always looks like a permanent record even if it catches the sun in the most whimsical of moods.

The photographs of the gardens of St Cloud are among the most famous of his works. By the time Atget photographed them they were already very decayed (a contemporary once said that Atget always seemed to be just one step ahead of the demolition crews) but it was in the gardens that he experimented most freely with his compositions and light effects, alternating between hard, mid-afternoon shadows and the gentle mists of dawn. It was in the gardens that he developed his innovative love of close-ups, staring down onto the roots of a tree or up into a crumbling statue's face. He loved playing with reflections and carefully balancing his compositions,

alvin langdon coburn

American/1882–1966

"If I admired the writing or expressed vision of any person, I was impelled to meet and photograph him."

Of the many factors contributing to Alvin Langdon Coburn's decision to pursue a career as an artist-photographer, possibly the most important was his meeting at the age of 18 with his cousin, Fred Holland Day. He was a leading pictorialist much influenced by the decadent movement and by the works of Oscar Wilde and Aubrey Beardsley.

Coburn was born in Boston in 1882. His father, a successful shirt manufac-turer, died in 1889, leaving his family sufficiently well provided for to enable Coburn to follow his later career without the commercial pressures he might have faced had he had to earn his living as a professional photographer. His mother, Fannie, was a keen and skilled amateur photographer and it was possibly under her influence that Coburn, who was given a camera at the age of eight, developed his earliest interest in photography.

84

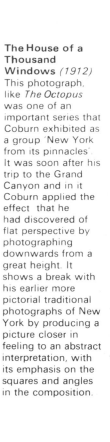

The House of a Thousand Windows *(1912)* This photograph, like *The Octopus* was one of an important series that Coburn exhibited as a group 'New York from its pinnacles'. It was soon after his trip to the Grand Canyon and in it Coburn applied the effect that he had discovered of flat perspective by photographing downwards from a great height. It shows a break with his earlier more pictorial traditional photographs of New York by producing a picture closer in feeling to an abstract interpretation, with its emphasis on the squares and angles in the composition.

Regent's Canal, London *(1904)* This is an example of Coburn's earlier soft focus pictorial work in which he sought to convey atmosphere rather than actuality. He concentrates on the effect of sunlight on water and on the overall harmonious design formed by the curve of the canal bridge and the buildings beyond. By waiting patiently for the precise moment when a canal barge and a horse moved into the composition, Coburn has produced a picture which sums up the scene.

Ezra Pound
(vortograph/1917)
Coburn's series of vortographs were the culmination of his interest in the abstract possibilities of photography.

Most of his vortographs are of inanimate objects such as glass or wood, but here Ezra Pound's profile is still recognizable.

86   When Coburn met Day in Boston in 1898, the latter was vying with STIEGLITZ for leadership of the pictorialist movement, the advocates of which believed that photographs should resemble paintings and that conscious effort should be exerted to achieve this effect. Day was planning to take an exhibition called 'The New School of American Pictorial Photography' to Britain. Coburn and his mother accompanied him, and in Britain Coburn met such leading pictorial workers as Frederick H Evans. A further trip with the exhibition to Paris in 1901 brought him into contact with other influential pictorialists – Frank Eugene and Robert Demachy. By 1903, Coburn had been elected to the two leading avant-garde groups of the time, Stieglitz's Photo-Secession in New York and the Linked Ring in London.

Coburn's main concession to pictorialism was in the use he made of the soft-focus lens, which gave his work, particularly his pictures of London and the River Thames, a misty romanticism reminiscent of Whistler, whose paintings he particularly admired. His landscape work was praised by Shaw for its ability always 'to convey a mood and not to impart local information'. Coburn, however, rejected the approach of pictorial photographers who, by drawing on negatives or applying colour or wash to prints to make them resemble pastels or wash drawings, produced a hybrid between photography and

graphic art. He preferred to use the complicated but entirely photographic gum-platinum process, in which a print was first made on platinum paper, a paper which was permanent and produced very subtle gradations of tone but not much intensity of shadow. This print was then coated with a thin layer of pigmented gum-bichromate which added a lustre and richness. When it was then replaced under the negative and re-exposed to light, the shadows were given the desired intensity but the tonal subtleties were still preserved.

In 1903, Coburn completed his photographic and artistic training by attending Arthur Dow's summer school at Ipswich, Massachusetts, where he studied the Japanese prints which were greatly to influence his ideas on design and composition. Earlier, Coburn had had some experience of working in Gertrude Käsebier's New York studio.

He set off for Britain with the intention of photographing the leading artists and writers of the day; 'If I admired the writing or expressed vision of any person,' he recalled in his autobiography, 'I was impelled to meet and photograph him.' George Bernard Shaw was the first subject he contacted, and the two men immediately established a rapport and friendship that helped Coburn gain introductions and resulted in Shaw's critical help whenever he exhibited his work. The first book of Coburn's portraits, *Men of Mark*, was published in 1913 and consisted of a bound series of hand-pulled photogravure plates. Coburn, who had studied the techniques of photogravure at the London County Council School of Photoengraving when in London between 1906 and 1909, prepared his own inks, experimented with various grades of paper and personally supervised the production of most of the plates for the series of books

Wyndham Lewis *(1916)* Photographed in the artist's London studio on 29 February, Wyndham Lewis was then leader of the avant-garde art group the Vorticists and editor of *Blast*. Coburn photographed him against one of his paintings in his studio in a deliberately defiant pose which echoes the angular content and structure of the painter's 'cubist' work. Coburn's contacts with Lewis and the Vorticists' critical champion Ezra Pound lead directly to his own pioneering invention and construction of the vortoscope to take abstract photographs. The picture is one of Coburn's best environmental portraits and was taken for inclusion in his 1922 publication *More Men of Mark*.

The Octopus *(1912)* Coburn entitled this view of the snow-covered Madison Gardens seen from the top of New York's Metropolitan Tower *The Octopus* because he felt the pattern achieved was more important than the subject matter. It is one of his earliest photographs showing the effect of modern, abstract art on his work and he later recalled in his autobiography that the composition was purely an exercise in filling a rectangular space with curves and masses.

he produced in this way.

Although Coburn photographed some of his sitters for *Men of Mark* in his rooms in Bloomsbury, the majority involved travel around the country. Where possible he used natural light, but he resorted to magnesium flash in dim interiors or on winter's days. He journeyed to Ireland in 1908 to photograph George Moore and William Butler Yeats. The latter portrait is one of his most successful, capturing an animation and 'mental alertness' (which Coburn always sought in his subjects) often lacking in some of his work. Coburn persuaded Yeats to recite some lines of his verse and, flaring off his magnesium flashlight at intervals, photographed Yeats while he did so.

Coburn's portraits of Henry James, whom he photographed first in New York and then again at his house at Rye in Sussex, resulted in one of his most important and creative commissions — to produce frontispiece illustrations to a 24-volume edition of James' collected works. For this Coburn travelled to France and Italy as well as accompanying James around London to select subjects.

Coburn's American photographs of 1911 and 1912, of industrial scenes in Pittsburg and of the Grand Canyon, show increasing tendencies towards abstraction. Back in New York in 1912, Coburn decided to use the odd perspectives he had found when photographing downwards into the Grand Canyon for a series of photographs he took from the tops of skyscrapers. Two of these, *The House of a Thousand Windows* and *The Octopus*, a view of Madison Square from the top of the Metropolitan Tower, were deliberate attempts to emulate the work of the avant-garde Cubist movement.

His interest in the possibilities of abstraction were further stimulated in 1916 by his meeting and photographing Wynd-ham Lewis, the leader of the Vorticists, for his *More Men of Mark* anthology. Ezra Pound, who had coined the name Vorticism for the movement, encouraged Coburn to construct a vortoscope to bring to photography the revolutionary possibilities of the art movement. The vortoscope was an instrument composed of three mirrors fastened together to produce effects similar to a kaleidoscope, the mirrors acting as a sort of prism splitting the image formed by the lens into segments. Most of the subjects he attempted with this contraption were pieces of wood or crystal, but he also made a very effective study of Pound's own distinctive profile. These pictures, together with some of Coburn's paintings in the Fauvist manner, were exhibited at the Camera Club in January 1917. Although Pound heralded them as a breakthrough, in the introduction he wrote to the exhibition catalogue, they were for the most part greeted with incomprehension. Moreover, the limited possibilities inherent in the idea meant that Coburn could not really pursue it.

In 1918 he moved to north Wales, taking up freemasonry and a general interest in mysticism with the same fervour with which he had once approached photography. Being far from his former artistic connections in London, he gradually lost touch and, although he returned to photography at intervals over the years until his death in 1966, his early creative work was never matched.

87

baron gayne de meyer

Demeyer Watson/Franco-British/c.1869–1946

**"He deliberately focuses his camera not upon
the sparkle of an eye but upon the light which
illuminates the eye."**
*(Observation on de Meyer in Camera Work
1914)*

The Baron de Meyer was an aesthete who brought a new lyricism to the areas of photography which attracted him. His innovations were to transform fashion photography from straightforward documentation to creative interpretation. He created poems of light from the most minimal of still-life compositions. His was the eye of the dandy *arriviste* who worked industriously to create an illusion of effortless grace as much in his own life style as in his seemingly ethereal images.

It is fitting that de Meyer's achievements should have been described by more than one commentator in musical terms. An article in *The Craftsman* (1914) explained 'He is bent, in fact, on translating his material into a fantasy of abstract beauty. It is almost a rendition of matter into music, wherein the notes are values and their relations and combinations form the harmonies.' To CECIL BEATON, writing

88

Mrs Rita de Acosta Lydig *(c.1913)* One of de Meyer's most celebrated portraits, this image is the photographic equivalent of the fashionable society portraits painted by the American-born artist John Singer Sargent. In this simple, soft-lit but striking composition, de Meyer has built his picture around the contrast of his subject's pale skin with her dark dress and hair and the dark, barely defined background.

Mrs Irene Castle modelling a Lewis hat *(1919)* This is one of the countless photographs taken by de Meyer for *Vogue* and a good example of the effective use of back-lighting to achieve a halo of light around his subject. De Meyer has succeeded in capturing the feathery lightness of an ostrich-adorned hat in a photograph the frivolity of which in no way detracts from the dramatic impact.

90 **Nijinsky in _Le Spectre de la Rose_** _(platinum print/ 1911)_ The magic of dance is perhaps one of the most elusive of the camera's subjects. Richard Buckle, in his 1979 biography of Diaghilev, wrote that 'Nobody who saw Nijinsky as the Rose ever got over it.' For those who did not see Nijinsky dance, however, he adds that 'The photographs of . . . de Meyer have perpetuated the magic of his interpretation.' This photograph was taken in Paris.

many years later, de Meyer was '. . . the Debussy of the camera.'

De Meyer came to photography at a time when crucial battles were being waged, led notably by ALFRED STIEGLITZ and his Photo-Secession group, to claim for photography its role as an art form. The Photo-Secessionists feared that the increasingly evident literalism of the camera, freed by faster films and easier manipulation, appeared to be robbing photography of that status. They pursued artistry through giving an impressionistic quality to their images. These achieved a painterly softness as if rendered in charcoal or pastel, rather than through the action of light on light-sensitive chemicals capable of high resolution. Such was the background which greeted de Meyer's first involvements in photography in the very early years of the century.

Stieglitz was de Meyer's first and most influential mentor, and it was in the pages of Stieglitz's prestigious quarterly _Camera Work_ that de Meyer published some of his earliest photographic essays. De Meyer took the Secessionist mode as the foundation of his style, a style which, through his refinements and embellishments, beautifully reconciled the painterly and the bewitchingly photographic. He further distinguished himself from the members of the more art-orientated Secessionist movement with his ties with the commercial worlds of fashion and beauty. Years later, looking back on his career, de Meyer was troubled by the idea that he had betrayed his art by becoming 'commercial'. It was to the now-elderly Stieglitz that he turned for reassurance. Stieglitz replied that he had '. . . often thought about you and the work you have done. The spirit in which I

feel you have lived. . . . No, you have not prostituted photography. Anyone who may say that or may have said that does not know what he or she is talking about.'

Little is known of the early years of de Meyer's life. It seems reasonable to assume that his snobbery threw a cloak of mystery over a background less illustrious than he felt appropriate to his role as a glittering socialite. This side of de Meyer's life began with his marriage to Olga Caracciolo in 1899. She served as a catalyst for his talents and, through her hazy connections with the Prince of Wales, opened the doors to society for her bedazzled partner. The historian Philippe Jullian has underlined the influence of Olga without whom he '. . . would have remained merely a fashionable decorator, or a snob who took photographs, or a homosexual ballet fan (and, indeed, he was all of these).'

Still-life with grapes *(1926)* The soft, dappled light of the bowl and its contents and the sequin sparkle of the foreground are typical de Meyer ingredients. The subject matter of his still-life studies is less the physical content of the images than the magical light which fills them.

91

Settled in a smart London home, the perfect couple entered the social whirl of the international aristocratic and artistic world. Olga was among the first and most stunning of an endless parade of society beauties and women of influence who considered it a privilege to be portrayed through de Meyer's lens. Among these were such celebrated figures as Rita de Acosta Lydig, portrayed by de Meyer in a pose strongly reminiscent of Sargent; the eccentric and strangely beautiful Marchesa Casati; the Hon Mrs Daisy Fellowes; Margot Asquith; Elsie de Wolfe and Gertrude Vanderbilt Whitney.

In the 1920s de Meyer's unique approach — a photographic concoction of a glamorized, highly stylized world of artifice, aestheticism and flawless, mysterious beauty — made him the *enfant chéri* of *Vogue* magazine. His fashion photographs,

society, stage, and screen portraits filled the pages of *Vogue* for many years, and, subsequently, those of *Harper's Bazaar*. By the time of Olga's death in 1931, however, the de Meyer style was being ousted by the work of a new generation of photographers, and in 1934 his contract with the publishers of *Harper's* was bluntly terminated. The last years of de Meyer's life, spent travelling in Europe before settling in the temperate climate of California, were not happy ones, and society took no further interest in what had been its most flattering photographic portraitist.

De Meyer's portraits are not character studies. They reveal nothing of the subjects save their vanity, superficial beauty and the photographer's intoxication with a world of fragile artifice and fantasy. They are, nonetheless, masterful images and de Meyer's innovative techniques used to

flatter his subjects have since become part of the basic vernacular of photography.

Soft side-lighting giving a moonlight effect, shimmering haloes of light achieved by back-lighting, the judicious disposition of reflective fabrics to create magical backgrounds, soft focus, the filtering of light through sheets of gauze — these are among the numerous techniques used by de Meyer to achieve results which have been described by Cecil Beaton: 'He used artificial light to make an aurora borealis. . . . His whites and silvers became dazzling, and the subtlety of his grey tones masterly. He invented a new universe: a high-key world of water sparkling with sunshine, of moonlight and candlelight, of water-lilies in glass bowls, of tissues and gauzes, of pearly lustre and dazzling sundrops filtered through blossoming branches.'

edward jean steichen

American/1879–1973

"The mission of photography is to explain man to man and each to himself. And that is the most complicated thing on earth."

Painter, photographer, curator — Edward Steichen, was a man of many talents and abilities. A founding member of the Photo-Secession, he helped to popularize photography both through his own work and by the organization of a wide variety of photographic exhibitions for the Museum of Modern Art in New York.

Steichen's interest in photography began in 1895, when, at the age of only 16, he acquired a second-hand box camera. Quickly frustrated by the lack of control and focus, he next bought a folding view camera, which used 4 × 5in glass plate negatives. At the time he was apprenticed as a designer for a lithographic firm, and was able to convince his superiors of the importance of photographs as a realistic basis for advertising posters. Steichen was encouraged to master photographic techniques, and many of the images he made were used by the firm. His early interest in photography as a useful means of communication was to continue throughout his career.

A general interest in art brought Steichen to consider the possibility of making artistic photographs. He began by trying to express his attraction to the mysterious atmosphere of moonlit landscapes in photography. In order to capture the moods he felt in the woods, Steichen experimented with exposure times and printing. Several accidents which occurred during exposure

Rodin, *Le Penseur* (1904) Steichen combined two negatives to make this successful portrait. First he photographed Rodin with his statue of Victor Hugo, and then he made a second exposure of *Le Penseur (The Thinker)*. Steichen printed the two negatives together as a tribute to the genius of Rodin, whom he greatly admired.

Cyclamen *(1905)* This portrait of Mrs Rita de Acosta Lydig was made by Steichen in New York when he was operating his highly successful portrait studio. The original was printed in gum-bichromate but it was published in gravure in *Camera Work* in 1914. Mrs Lydig was a well-known, extravagant socialite with an extreme fondness for white flowers. This portrait exudes both luxury and sensuality.

93

94 **Heavy Roses**
(1914) This picture
was made near
Steichen's home in
Voulangis. The
original was a
palladium print. The
palladium process
was similar to the
platinum process
but palladium was
substituted for the
more expensive
metal. Both types of
print were more
stable than the
silver print. They
also produced a
wide range of subtle
grey tones well
suited for rendering
the subject here.

provided him with the means to achieve certain effects, as when a camera lens, spattered with rain, created a diffused image. The same effect was produced when the camera tripod was accidentally kicked during a long exposure. Steichen also occasionally photographed a scene purposefully out of focus. To emphasize the desired mood further, Steichen learned to make gum-bichromate prints. This was a pigment process by which a sheet of paper was coated with a combination of watercolour and gum arabic, and made sensitive to the light by bichromate of potash. After exposure to a negative, the paper was floated on a water bath and the parts of the image unaffected by light were washed away. This technique was perfect for representing large grainy masses of dark and light, and an added benefit was the multiplicity of colours afforded by varying the tints of pigment used. Several printings on one sheet were possible in different tints. Steichen used the gum-bichromate process to great effect, and romantic, mood-laden, painterly images formed the bulk of his early non-commercial work.

When he had reached 21, after having exhibited in several salons, Steichen decided to go to Europe. Armed with camera, paints, and a letter of introduction to ALFRED STIEGLITZ, he left his home in Milwaukee. The Camera Club of New York was Steichen's first stop. There he met Stieglitz, who admired his work and purchased three prints at five dollars each. After several months in Paris, Steichen went to London in order to submit some of his photographs to exhibitions of the Royal Photographic Society and the Linked Ring. Fred Holland Day, a leading American photographer, was organizing a show called 'The New School of American Photography', and he selected 21 of Steichen's prints. The exhibition proved to be controversial, and included most of the leaders of the pictorial movement, with the exception of Stieglitz, who for some reason refused to become involved. The London critics made much of the show, and Steichen's reputation was assured.

He returned to Paris and began a series of portraits of prominent creative figures. Perhaps the most successful work of this period is Rodin's portrait. A combination of two negatives, Steichen first photographed Rodin with his statue of Victor Hugo, and then made a second exposure of Le Penseur (The Thinker). The two negatives were printed together, and the resultant dramatic image is Steichen's tribute to the genius of Rodin.

In 1902 Steichen decided to return to New York, where he opened a professional portrait studio at 291 Fifth Avenue. It soon became a social necessity to be photographed by Steichen, and among his sitters were Eleonora Duse and J Pierpont Morgan. The Morgan portrait was so unflatteringly realistic that Morgan, used to heavily re-touched, idealized images of himself, tore it up. Today however, the Morgan portrait is striking in its suggestion of ruthless power. With the formation of the Photo-Secession and the subsequent establishment of the periodical Camera Work and the gallery '291', Steichen was able to indulge his interest in and knowledge of contemporary art by organizing exhibitions. He put together shows of Rodin drawings and Cezanne watercolours, and generally encouraged Stieglitz to show more non-photographic contemporary work.

In 1906, tired of his portrait business, Steichen returned to Paris. There he began to experiment with a small hand camera, and also made some highly successful autochromes. Introduced by the Lumière company, autochromes were the forerunners of today's colour transparencies, and produced a positive colour image on a glass plate. Steichen's autochromes were later reproduced in colour in Camera Work.

During the First World War Steichen supervised aerial photographic operations for the American Army. His experiences during the war led him to give up painting and eschew the soft, romanticized, pictorial images he had been producing. He began to experiment with realistic representation, and as an exercise made over 1000 different negatives of a white cup and saucer, exploring all its photographic possibilities. From 1923 to 1938 Steichen was Condé Nast's chief photographer. His portraits of motion picture and theatrical celebrities and fashion photographs appeared regularly in Vogue and Vanity Fair. Steichen also worked in advertising, and his photographs from that period are models of slick professionalism.

Although he was in his sixties, Steichen ran a photographic unit for the American Navy during the Second World War. He covered naval aviation and ultimately was placed in charge of all naval combat photography. In 1947 Steichen was made director of the Department of Photography of the Museum of Modern Art in New York, and did much to bring the medium to the public's attention by organizing vast popular exhibitions such as 'The Family of Man'. In addition, he showed the work of such artists as WALKER EVANS, CARTIER-BRESSON, BRASSAI and WESTON.

Steichen's final photographic project, begun in 1959, was an extended colour motion picture study of a tree in the grounds of his home in Connecticut. The recipient of hundreds of awards and honours, Edward Steichen died in 1973.

95

august sander
German/1876–1964

A fortuitous encounter with a stranger led August Sander to create a collection of photographic portraits of enduring value and interest. Unrivalled in scope, the *People of the Twentieth Century* was an unfinished record of the German people in which Sander catalogued a multitude of physical types and occupations. Sander's achievement was an inspiration to contemporary photographers like Diane Arbus and RICHARD AVEDON.

Born in 1876, Sander worked beside his father in a mining community from a young age. But an opportunity to assist a landscape photographer who wanted to take pictures of the countryside around the mine influenced Sander's choice of a future career. With characteristic resolve, Sander determined to obtain a camera and master the art of photography in his spare time. Reluctantly encouraged by his family, and with the help of a wealthy uncle, Sander acquired a 13 × 18cm camera and a darkroom, housed in a small hut next to a barn. Sander's first subjects were the family next door. He arranged the group and exposed a good negative, but had some trouble with the prints. After trial and error, Sander managed to master the use of printing-out-paper, which produced a positive image after exposure with a negative to daylight and was then toned and fixed to stop development. Although his first sitters were not pleased with the results (which were less than flattering), Sander continued his investigations into the medium. He made his first sales when his fellow-workers at the mine ordered about 70 copies of a group portrait. His reputation spread quickly, and soon he was fulfilling portrait commissions for the many young Germans who were emigrating to America and wanted to leave mementoes behind for their families.

In 1896 Sander was conscripted into the German Army, and when he was off-duty he assisted a commercial photographer who made military souvenir portraits. After his war service, Sander travelled throughout Germany, apprenticing himself to prominent photographers. He added architectural and advertising photography to his already considerable skills, and also briefly studied portrait painting in Dresden. After his marriage in 1901, Sander left Germany for Austria, where he first worked as an assistant and then purchased a studio. He began to produce highly re-touched images in gum-bichromate, and the demand for his work grew. Experimentation with natural colour techniques led to the purchase of prints by the Leipzig Museum as well as awards from international exhibitions. Although the studio was successful, Sander soon found himself in financial difficulty because of

"If he photographed the blind children, the unemployed, cretins and cripples, it was with a gentleness and benign sympathy."
(Cecil Beaton)

his rapidly developing taste for paintings, books and antiques.

Because of the bad health of his eldest son, Erich, in 1909 Sander moved the family to Cologne, where he opened another studio. For some time he had been formulating a new approach to portraiture – one which would release the genre from its static conventions. Sander began to feel that studio surroundings restricted individuality and that technical problems outside the studio's confines (such as uncontrolled lighting) could be surmounted. In order to pursue these ideas, Sander began to make weekend excursions into his native district, the Westerwald. Riding an old bicycle, a rucksack filled with photographic equipment and samples of his work on his back, he went in search of new subjects. The peasants of the Wester-

The Notary *(1925)* This photograph of Dr Quinke, a notary in Cologne, is noted for the inclusion of the Doctor's magnificent dog and the curious manner in which neither of the two are looking at the camera. Sander always tried to maintain an impartial distance from his sitters.

The Varnisher *(1932)* This image is one of the series *Trades, Classes and Professions*. Sander wanted to photograph representatives of every profession and social strata in pre-war Germany. Though he claimed he was only interested in types, the character of the individual comes through clearly.

wald proved willing and Sander spent a year photographing them in their native surroundings. This series was the start of *People of the Twentieth Century*. Sander returned to the German Army during the First World War, while his wife ran the studio. Immediately following the war Sander was kept busy taking photographs for compulsory identification cards.

Sander had many friends in artistic circles, and some of them took great interest in his work. He became particularly close to the Marxist painter Franz Wilhelm Seiwart, who believed that art should reflect the structures of society. Discussions with Seiwart gave Sander the impetus to continue and expand the Westerwald project, but with one crucial difference. Objectivity became the key to Sander's approach. He refused to impose his beliefs or prejudices on his sitters, yet the printing techniques he used produced unreal pictorial images. Intent and technique were at odds. Sander made an enlargement of a Westerwald portrait on a glossy paper ordinarily used for technical photographs. Suddenly every detail was revealed and the portrait gained impact and immediacy. Although unflattering and almost totally non-commercial, the picture fulfilled Sander's ideals and, giving up pictorialism, he began to add to his collection with enthusiasm. Members of every profession passed before Sander's camera, and all were recorded with clarity and attention to telling detail. He thought of his subjects as archetypes, timeless examples of the essences of humanity and he photographed judges and chefs, painters and secretaries, businessmen, musicians and circus performers.

In collaboration with the novelist Alfred Döblin, in 1929 Sander published *Antlitz der Zeit* (*Faces of Our Time*), a selection of 60 portraits with an accompanying text. This was to have been the forerunner of a more ambitious project, but, as the Nazis came to power, Sander's position became uncertain. His son Erich was a member of the Socialist Workers Party and, in 1934, was arrested and imprisoned by the Gestapo. Sander's archives were ransacked, and later that year all available stocks of *Antlitz der Zeit* were confiscated and the printing plates destroyed. The family left Cologne for the Westerwald and Sander stopped work on his project. He developed an interest in less controversial subjects and began to photograph landscapes.

Sander was never to complete *People of the Twentieth Century*. By the end of the war his age prevented him from making new portraits. Instead, he devoted himself to reprinting and cataloguing old negatives, arranging exhibitions and teaching. He died in 1964.

jacques-henri lartigue

French/born 1894

"I take photographs with love, so I try to make them art objects. But I make them for myself first and foremost – that is important."

'Photography is a magic thing! A magic thing with all sorts of mysterious smells, a bit strange and frightening, but something you learn to love very quickly!' wrote Jacques-Henri Lartigue in his diary in 1901. He was seven years old, and had just begun a love affair with the camera that continues to the present. Lartigue's father gave him his first camera that same year and he was soon writing, 'I know very well that many, many things are going to ask me to have their pictures taken and I will take them all.'

Lartigue was born into a large and prosperous French family. His father was a businessman, and recreation was apparently the family's main pursuit. Jacques-Henri faithfully described the family's pleasures both in his diary and with his camera. The Lartigues and their friends were particularly enamoured with motion; they built gliders and sail-powered bobsleighs, attended hot air balloon races and motor car rallies. Aeroplanes were also another major preoccupation. Jacques-Henri's sense of timing was impeccable, and he was often able to capture his subjects in mid-flight. As he had no preconceptions about photography, he was able to look at his surroundings with a fresh sensibility. Anything was possible, and many of Lartigue's most entertaining images were pictures in which logical motion was temporarily arrested. Glimpses of animals and humans caught in charmingly unlikely poses are poignant mementoes of a vanished world, and all the more fascinating for having been captured by a child.

As a young man, Lartigue's interest in machines was partly supplanted by a growing awareness of the opposite sex. He would often sit alongside a footpath in the Bois de Boulogne, surreptitiously waiting for the right moment in which to snatch a portrait of an elegantly dressed Parisienne passing by. The fear of being caught in the act by his unknowing models (or their male companions) was far exceeded by the pleasure of adding more pictures to his collection. Lartigue was attracted as much by their outrageously extravagant hats and ensembles as by their faces, and his photographs are an entertaining record of the fashions of the day.

**The Pavillon
Dauphine** *(1912)*
99
As a young man
Lartigue often
wandered through
the Bois de
Boulogne, taking
photographs of
passers-by who
caught his eye.
Although his most
frequent subjects
were beautiful
women, Lartigue
made this picture of
a young
equestrienne and
her teacher in front
of the Pavillon
Dauphine. The
picture records, from
the insider's view-
point, a way of life
that was to vanish
with the coming of
the First World War.

From 1914 to 1918 Lartigue used his camera to document another way of life, that of wartime. He served as a staff driver and recorded scenes of Paris before and after the Armistice. The year after the war ended Lartigue married Bibi Messager, who became his favourite subject. During the course of their marriage Bibi was seen in London, at exercise class, on the beach, dancing the tango and with their son.

Lartigue began to experiment with moving pictures in 1910, when his father gave him his very first cinecamera. Four years later his films were being bought by Pathe and used in newsreels. Lartigue also experimented with autochromes, and with stereoscopic, view, and hand-held cameras. Since the beginning of the 1950s Lartigue has worked extensively with colour transparencies.

Concurrent with his photography, Lartigue has been a prolific diarist and painter. In fact, he has always thought of himself as a painter foremost, and only began to exhibit his photographs seriously in the mid-1950s. He began keeping a journal in 1900, and filled volumes with descriptions of daily routine, philosophical musings, and technical details about his varied visual pursuits. As a child he would often sketch the scenes he photographed, in case something went wrong in the darkroom. He also made albums of his photographs, arranging them in sequence and with accompanying captions. Lartigue has filled over 110 albums, and in 1979 he gave his entire body of work to France.

Lartigue photographed the daily life of a very privileged class from the inside. The fact that he was a friend to nearly all of his subjects gives his pictures warmth and intimacy. Highly personal and made for his own enjoyment, Lartigue's work is unsurpassed in its evocation of a life spent in the pursuit of sunshine, friendship, and pleasure.

100

Portrait of Zissou *(1905)*
At the age of 11, Lartigue made this photograph of his elder brother Zissou, whose athletic prowess and inventive curiosity made him a natural ringleader and photographic subject. Lartigue's quick instincts and a fast shutter speed enabled him to freeze action and capture Zissou's high spirits and vitality on film.

Portrait of Renée Perle *(1930)*
In 1930 Lartigue began a romantic relationship with Renée Perle during which he produced hundreds of photographs. In August of that year he made this picture of Mme Perle at the pool of the Chambre d'Amour in Biarritz. By careful organization of light, shadow and reflective water, Lartigue produced a harmoniously balanced, stylish glamour of the Thirties.

emil otto hoppé

British/1878–1972

"Hoppé was unique in that his work showed him to be a man of rarefied politeness, of cultured background and a collector of distinction." *(Cecil Beaton)*

From 1910 until 1920, Emil Otto Hoppé was one of the best known and most commercially successful portrait photographers in London. Born in Munich in 1878 and educated in Vienna, Hoppé came to London around 1900, and met and became friendly with an influential group of amateur photographers which included Furley Lewis, J C Warburg and A L COBURN. Coburn in particular stimulated his interest in photography as a means of artistic ex-

pression, and from 1903 Hoppé's amateur work met with increasing success. When at last the prize money won from photographic competitions almost equalled his salary at the bank where he worked, he became convinced that his portraiture could be commercially viable. In 1907 Hoppé opened his own studio, determined to break from the stilted conventions of Edwardian photography and aiming for a new simplicity and naturalness.

102

Lady Lavery and her attendant
(1914) This portrait is of Hazel Martyn, the American-born second wife of the leading portrait painter Sir John Lavery.
The little Arab boy was part of the Lavery's household in Tangier. The photograph is a conscious attempt to produce a 'camera-portrait' as a modern day equivalent to the style of portraiture adopted in the seventeenth and eighteenth centuries by the Dutch portraitists Sir Peter Lely or Sir Godfrey Kneller. The slight use of soft focus enhances this painterly effect. The picture is lit from the right and taken on Kodak flat cellulose film. The lighting is probably a 1000 watt flood partially reflected using an exposure of one to two seconds.

Arnold Bennett
(1911) This portrait of the writer Arnold Bennett was one of a series taken of British men of letters which established Hoppé's reputation as a portraitist. Lit from the left using natural light, the photograph was probably taken on a 12 × 10in studio camera with a Dallmeyer Portrait lens. The use and inclusion of the sitter's hand and cigarette created an important compositional device as well as breaking new ground in showing a sitter in an informal and relaxed pose.

Hoppé believed that he could capture the true essence of his sitters' personalities only by what he termed the 'thawing process' to which ends he would talk to his sitters at length, trying to put them at ease and establish a rapport. With carefully chosen furniture and decoration, he created the atmosphere of a restful drawing room, keeping his lighting equipment to a minimum and using a 10 × 8in reflex camera that could be operated unobtrusively with a cable release. Hoppé would first study the sitter, watching for characteristic expressions or gestures. Then, when he judged the psychological moment to have come, he would release the shutter. During an average successful sitting he would usually make no more than six exposures on half plate or 10 × 8in glass negatives.

Hoppé's early portraits are marked by their insight and the bold simplicity of their design; at the time, many of Hoppé's portraits seemed remarkably informal. His backgrounds are usually plain, and if any props are used, they are carefully chosen to add symmetry and strength to the composition: a single framed print hangs on the wall behind Leon Bakst; Edmund Gosse sits at a plain table, a vase of crocuses placed before him; Edward Gordon Craig stands in profile looking pensively downwards, his hands in his trouser pockets; Somerset Maugham half smiling, leans casually on the back of a wooden chair, a cigarette held between his fingers. The use of a sitter's hands as a compositional device was a favourite trait in many of Hoppé's portraits, and in his study of Arnold Bennett the prominently held cigarette in Bennett's raised hand gives balance and immediacy.

Although Hoppé worked mainly in his studio, he also undertook a number of *in situ* or 'at home' portraits. His photograph of the sculptor Epstein, taken in 1911 in the artist's Chelsea studio, is particularly successful in the way Epstein is shown half-length, looking directly out at the viewer as a counterpoint to the profile of the sphinx behind him. When photographing Henry James at his house in Rye, Hoppé used the light coming from the library window, reflected by a sheet of white paper stretched on a drawing board to give roundness to James' strongly-lit profile. Hoppé's finished photographs were characteristically rich in tone with a subtle, velvety texture which is often lost in reproduction. The presentation of the print mounted on two shades of brown card and signed by the photographer added to the final arresting effect.

In 1910 Hoppé held his first one-man exhibition at the Royal Photographic Society, London, and the subsequent four-page supplement printed by the *Illustrated London News* heralded his emergence as an important portrait photographer. In 1911 he moved to a larger studio. Here, with an exclusive contract with Diaghilev, he made portraits of all the leading members of the Ballet Russe appearing in London at the time. Although constrained by the relatively long exposures required, he succeeded in conveying the drama and spectacle of the dancers and the exoticism of Bakst's costumes.

In 1913 Hoppé moved yet again, to a 27-roomed house in London that had once been the home of the portrait painter Sir John Everett Millais. In the years following, Hoppé became best known for his portraits of women, including the leading society beauties and actresses of the day such as Lady Lavery and Lady Diana Cooper, whose portraits were much in demand by magazines such as *Tatler* and *Sketch*. Hoppé continued to make many fine portraits during the war years, but increasingly the demands of commercialism led him to resort to time-saving methods and extensive re-touching, and he began to seek fresh creative stimuli. By the 1920s he started to direct his energies towards travel and topographical photography.

Although Hoppé's landscape work was never 'pictorial' in the manner of Coburn, it was at first essentially romantic and lyrical in style. For his book *Picturesque Great Britain*, published in 1926, he photographed the British countryside and villages, recording with nostalgia and affection a traditional way of life that was vanishing under a tide of industrialization. In *Romantic America* of 1927, his interpretation when faced with the dramatic skylines of the new cities begins to take on a more geometric, harder edge, though tempered with a certain softness. Hoppé wrote, 'I felt that in the hard angles and uncompromising verticals [of the new architecture] dwelt the spirit of a new romance.' He searched for unusual angles and perspectives to convey the stern grandeur he saw around him. He photographed skyscraper walls rising from dark streets, illuminated like cliff-faces in the sunlight; he leaned perilously from high windows to take pictures of workmen on girders at dizzying heights; he photographed the Manhattan skyline through the girders of Brooklyn Bridge, showing it dwarfed behind latticed metal work.

In the late 1920s and throughout the 1930s until the outbreak of the Second World War, Hoppé continued his travels, compiling material — usually using a Rollieflex or Leica — for books and articles based on extensive visits to India, Australia, New Zealand, Bali, Indonesia, Africa and, in Europe, Bavaria, Poland and Czechoslovakia. Most of this work was competent, occasionally interesting, but not often outstanding.

Perhaps the most creative work of this period was his industrial photography, in which he became one of the pioneers of the 'modern' approach. In 1928 he photographed extensively scenes of British industry. Along with his general studies of forests of cranes silhouetted against the skyline, Hoppé isolated details such as a ship's propellers or, in juxtaposition with rough wooden stakes, huge lengths of steel anchor chain, exploring their texture as they lay beneath the riveted underbelly of a huge ship. At the end of 1928 he went to Germany to take pictures for his most impressive book of industrial photography, *Deutsche Arbeit (Germany at Work)* published in 1930. In this he portrayed a fully industrialized, urban society. It was strangely de-populated but powerfully realized, showing the Borsig Locomotive works, the steel foundries at Essen, atmospheric studies of cauldrons of molten ore, and unadorned storage tanks outside Berlin. In one of these photographs Hoppé frames his picture so as to place a finely-wrought spiral staircase in the centre which stands in relief and links the two vast tanks on either side, whose outer edges spread out of the composition. Once again, Hoppé's ability to see and select with his photographic eye harks back to the strength of his best portraits.

After the war Hoppé devoted his time to running a picture agency, but until his death in 1972 maintained an active interest in the progress and applications of photography.

Berlin oil tanks *(1928)* One of a series, this photograph was taken for the book *Deutsche Arbeit (Germany at Work)* showing the outward manifestations of reconstructed German industry. It is one of the earliest deliberate attempts at commercial photography and combines modern ideas of the new realism school of photography with older pictorialist concepts. The deliberate framing, cropping and use of shadow, by concentrating on a detail such as the spiral staircase, conveys a general symmetry. Hoppé probably took this with a Graflex quarter plate camera.

edward weston
American/1886–1958

> **"An excellent conception can be quite obscured by faulty technical execution or clarified by faultless technique."**

Edward Weston made some of photography's best-known pictures. In 1927 he photographed a glowing nautilus shell on a dark ground, and the resultant image is both compact and intricate. In 1930 he based a number of pictures on green peppers taken in close-up; these images resemble nothing so much as writhing muscles. A halved artichoke head makes a picture as delicately patterned as any late Gothic ceiling. A cabbage leaf cascades like frozen water. Pale toadstools make strong visceral shapes in the darkness. He was able to uncover an extraordinary visual drama even in commonplace items.

Born in 1886, Weston was four years older than PAUL STRAND and a generation ahead of ANSEL ADAMS, who was impressed and influenced by Weston's photography in the late 1920s. Brought up in Chicago, he moved to California in 1906, where he worked for the rest of his life with the

106

Toadstool *(1931)*
Weston returned from Mexico to California in 1928, and in 1929 he moved to Carmel, where he made many of his famous close-up pictures of peppers and kelp. He believed that intense scrutiny of natural forms would reveal the truth, echoing similar views expressed in the nineteenth century by Pre-Raphaelite artists such as William Holman Hunt. Weston's pictures of animal life loom large, filling the frame. Hardly intended as botanical studies, they invade consciousness and suggest states of mind — darkly disturbed or perfectly at ease, according to the angle of approach and choice of lighting.

exception of long periods in Mexico in the 1920s. He became a pictorialist in the soft-focus style popular around 1900. By 1920 Weston had begun to experiment with new styles and subjects; he made fragment-photographs of nudes, and, shortly afterwards, pictures of industrial details. Late in 1922 he paid a long visit to New York, where he met ALFRED STIEGLITZ, Paul Strand and Charles Sheeler, a painter who had made purist, sharp-focus pictures of

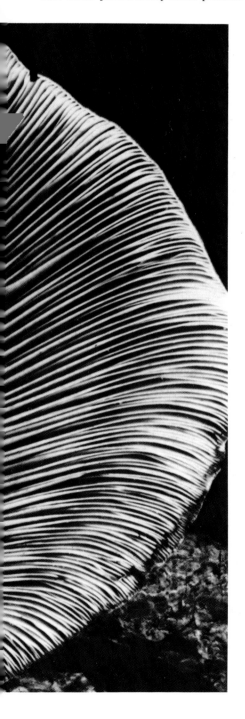

architecture as early as 1917. Weston did not count this trip to New York as especially formative. In 1923 he moved to Mexico with the former screen-actress and future revolutionary Tina Modotti. He remained in Mexico until 1925, and it was during this period that he established his photographic style and philosophy: '... the camera should be used for a recording of *life*, for rendering the very substance and quintessence of the *thing itself*, whether it be polished steel or palpitating flesh.'

There is, however, a marked paradox in Weston's art. He is a 'straight' photographer in the manner of Stieglitz, who advised him, in 1922, to aim for 'a maximum of simplification with a maximum of detail'. At the same time there is no avoiding the fact that his is an emphatically personal art. Paul Strand disliked modern society and its utilitarian values. He disliked it in general, whereas Weston objected in particular – and especially to that Californian society around Los Angeles in which he had to earn his living. In Mexico he responded to the vitality of the place and its customs. In his diaries, which he kept through most of his working life, he left a full record of his responses to people and places. He sought out experiences which brought acute and sometimes harsh self-knowledge. Writing of his liking for bull-fighting he refers to 'those fearful forbidden heights from which some see beauty masked and arrayed in alien guise'.

He associated with people who, like himself, knew, and took pictures of, the Mexican painters José Clemente Orozco and Diego Rivera, and presented them as fierce, inspired creatures. Tina Modotti, who was to become a well-known photographer in her own right, he pictured as a resolute and beautiful heroine. He saw other Mexican friends in the same extreme light: the heroic head of Guadelupe Marin de Rivera, whose 'walk was like a panther's'; the Colt-toting General Manuel Hernandez Galvan, later shot dead by assassins.

Where Paul Strand imagined a world of heroic country people, Weston pictured exultant heroes and heroines, creatures of impulse who lived life to the full. This was Weston's theme, and it pervades all his pictures, whether they are of wind-blown dunes, weathered stumps of trees, opulent female nudes or fertile landscapes. To succeed it was necessary to respond emotionally to the subject: 'I do not consciously compose, I make my negative entirely under the effect of my emotion in response to a given subject. I do not stop to analyse composition even in print. I saw a thing

well or I did not see it.' In other words, to photograph was to test his capacity to respond; and successful pictures were evidence of his adequacy in the face of the world's beauty.

His photographic career was a quest. It resulted in moments of great composure, embodied most fully in the graceful range of forms and tones assembled in the nautilus shells. It resulted in visions of landscape which are as beautiful as any taken by an American photographer. *Eel River Ranch*, 1937, has a balance of the kind which Ansel Adams so often achieved. Yet he took many photographs which are more troubling than reassuring. The giant peppers which writhe out of darkness in 1930 are expressive; they hint at a disturbed inner state, as does the coiled kelp which he pictured in the same year. These, and many other images, are forms which express troubled states of mind. It is fitting that an artist dependent on emotional response should explore such extremes of turbulence and darkness. His photographer-contemporaries in Germany interpreted nature in much the same way; and they too were purists, working with an objective medium which scarcely seemed to allow the self to intrude.

At a deeper level Weston's work is an exploration of the senses and the death of the senses. Engrossed by palpitating flesh and by lush vegetation, he was inevitably conscious of the opposite, of death, ruin and desiccation. He photographed bare sand among the dunes at Oceano, dried timbers in the mountains and on Point Lobos (his favourite site, on the Californian coast), cacti in the deserts, ruined farmsteads and urban wastelands. In 1941 he travelled through the south and east of the United States, taking pictures to illustrate an edition of Walt Whitman's *Leaves of Grass*. He focused on the abandoned plantations of Louisiana and on the cemeteries of New Orleans, and seems to have been much obsessed by death.

Weston confronted, and was confronted by nature. Many of his landscapes end in barriers of rock. By contrast, those of Ansel Adams usually roll unbroken into the far distance. However, Weston never relents; cacti, boulders, stumps of trees rise up against him; fences, thickets, screens of timber cut off any relief to be found in a distant view; he deals continually in extremes, of beauty and of dereliction. He always seems to wonder about himself, his adequacy, his joys and his mortality. In 1958 he died of Parkinson's Disease. He was, without doubt, a major, if paradoxical, artist, a puritan in love with the body of the world.

107

paul strand
American/1890–1976

" In a sense the artist should not be asked for the philosophy of life upon which he bases his work. The work is <u>the thing itself</u>."

Paul Strand is one of the heroes of modern photography. In 1917 he was honoured by ALFRED STIEGLITZ who devoted a full issue of the meticuluously printed magazine *Camera Work* to his photographs. In his introduction, Stieglitz, who spent his life rooting out nonsense, praised Strand extravagantly as 'someone who has actually done something from within' and 'added something to what has gone before'. Nothing worthwhile, Stieglitz thought, had been done in photography in the three or four years prior to 1917.

Paul Strand was born in New York City in 1890. As a student of the documentary photographer Lewis Hine at the Ethical Culture High School after 1907, Strand made photographs which were, in Stieglitz's words, 'the direct expression of today'. His pictures of 1917 are unusually diverse, and, more importantly, foretell much of what was to follow in photography. He took candid pictures of 'street-people', including a cab driver and a beggar, who seem to reveal their secrets and anxieties, and show how Strand anticipated the psychological realism of photographers such as ANDRE KERTESZ and HENRI CARTIER-BRESSON in the 1930s. Unfortunately, he seems never again to have taken pictures of this sort.

In 1917, Strand published a series of photographs taken from unusual angles, one of which shows shadows cast by girders and two small figures in the shade by the edge of the road illustrating Strand's interest in individuals and their relationships with the dominating geometry of modern architecture. Strand's New Yorkers maintain a forceful presence even though dwarfed by the tall buildings of the city. They precede, by a full decade, the same adamant citizens who gestured their way through MOHOLY-NAGY's European city squares in the late 1920s.

Some of these early pictures have little to do with candidness or dominating urban geometry; in the main they raise visual problems, and are difficult to gauge. Strand chose, and continued to choose, viewpoints which obscured as much as they revealed. While it is possible, after looking over these images, to be reasonably certain of angles, boundaries and volumes, this information has to be worked

Wall Street *(1915)*   109
Strand's early
pictures are mainly
of urban subjects.
He represented city
buildings as
systematic and
massive, as in this
picture of pedestrians
passing by the
façade of a bank.
His citizens are
dwarfed, but
resolute — each
makes a distinctive
shape. Strand was
concerned to resist
dehumanizing forces
in modern life, and
through pictures
such as this he
sought to find an
image to stand for
individual life
surviving, and even
flourishing, in mass
society.

110 for. Strand deliberately conceals co-ordinates, throws the ground into shadow or screens it altogether. From the outset, his pictures contained odd dislocations and gaps between principal surfaces which have to be bridged by the imagination. Thus Strand returns the onlooker to an acute awareness of seeing as an active process, constituted both by surmise and direct apprehension.

Strand continued to be absorbed by the act of seeing throughout his life. No matter where he worked, in New Mexico or the Hebrides, he found spatial difficulties around which to organize his pictures. None of his contemporaries were so obsessed by vision; yet the obsession was long-standing. Nineteenth-century artists devoted themselves to the scrutiny of nature, for in nature lay the natural laws to which man is indebted. In such circumstances, to see clearly is to understand fundamentally, and thus the higher the level of consciousness, the better. Strand wrote vigorously on such matters between 1917 and 1923, and expressed his admiration for 'the purely direct photographs of Stieglitz' and 'a new and living act of vision'. He was bitterly opposed to the mechanized and utilitarian present, and instead proposed a contemplative life in communion with nature. His photographs, most of which require prolonged study, initiate the viewer into the contemplative life which he recommends.

At the same time, and perhaps inevit-ably, Strand had great respect for things as they are. In 1923 he said to Stieglitz, 'Notice how every object, every blade of grass is felt and accounted for, the full acceptance and use of the thing in front of it'. To express this attitude he sometimes worked with sets of comparable items. In 1916 he photographed *The White Fence* at Port Kent, New York. At first sight, the picture looks like nothing more than a barrier composed of identical slats, but, as it was photographed from close range, it is possible to see that these apparently identical elements have weathered differently. He took pictures of doorways, façades, symmetrical artefacts; always there are significant differences from left to right. Strand only admits particulars, and, like many of his contemporaries, photographed grasses, ferns and leaves. Here too he is careful to show that these exist in particular places at particular times. Strand's grasses often dip under the weight of dew, or twist into and out of light, thus acknowledging a greater world of which they are but fragments.

Yet Strand is possibly even better known as a portraitist. He made portraits wherever he went – in New York in 1916, in Mexico in the early 1930s, on the Gaspé peninsula in Canada during 1936, in New England during the 1940s, and then in the Hebrides, Italy, France, Egypt and Ghana. No other photographer celebrated such handsome and dignified people. Generally country folk, Strand's

The White Fence, Port Kent *(1916)* This is one of Strand's most famous early pictures. The line of slats suggests uniformity, but each upright has been weathered and broken differently – there is variety within conformity. The picture may also have its symbolic side, in that a domain of light stands out from a dark background. Certainly the invitation to discriminate among apparently similar elements recurs in his pictures.

STRAND

Archie MacDonald *(1954)*
After a brief spell working in New York, Strand rarely photographed in urban and industrial settings. He preferred agrarian, or at least traditional, communities, and he liked to make frontal portraits of this kind. Such frontality implies respect and integrity; it also means that Strand has not taken advantage of his subjects, who appear fully self-conscious. Yet as they present themselves Strand's people reveal their own ideas of decorum. Archie MacDonald is posing simply as himself, dignified and impassive.

111

subjects seem to be at one with nature; and the older they get the more this seems to be the case.

Strand's people look at the camera as an agent acting for posterity, and those young or naïve enough look out respectfully or with their best face forward. Others, those getting on in years or involved in daily tasks, pay little heed. They exist in, and support society through, the present moment, and leave it to the less responsible to dream about other times. His country people are from an age-old agrarian culture, superior to the mechanized world which Strand deplored.

These grave fisherfolk and farmers are close kin to the heroes and heroines of labour who are met everywhere in the documentary photography of the 1930s.

The difference is that Strand does not find a few anonymous, representative figures. Susan Thompson of Cape Split, Maine, or Mr Bennett of Vermont present themselves as individuals.

Strand discovered communities worthy of respect wherever he travelled, and he left evidence of an eye which cherished even the most ordinary of subjects. In his books, *Time in New England* (1950), *Un Paese* (1955), *Tir a'Mhurain* (1962) and *Living Egypt* (1969), he both reported on the present and envisaged a time when mankind might live in harmony with nature. Strand grew up during a period in which great hopes were invested in the future. His mentor, Alfred Stieglitz, battled resolutely towards this better future, and Strand continued his work.

weegee

Arthur H Fellig/Polish-born American/1899–1969

"All over the world people ask me what is the secret of your formula? I just laugh; I have no formula, I'm just myself."

'Weegee – the Famous', self-styled 'World's Greatest Photographer' would surely have elicited smiles of incredulity if encountered in the pages of cheap crime fiction of the 1930s or 1940s. Yet this larger-than-life character was for real – tough, cynical, cocky, shabby, but above all, human. His best photographs present a unique insight into the seamier facets of New York life. They are images of violence and of tragedy, of hardship, suffering and the bizarre.

They are very often photographs which required guts, tenacity and diplomacy on the part of the photographer, but Weegee was fearless, completely devoted to his task and he trod boldly and promptly where less assured photographers would so often have held back. They are photographs filled with life and emotion and Weegee's humanity provides the necessary counterpoint to his voyeurism.

Born in Poland in 1899, Weegee, whose

112

Tenement fire
(1942) Weegee has captured the essence of a human tragedy by concentrating on the tortured faces of the two women whose loved ones have perished in the fire. Neither the flames, nor the destruction which they have caused are shown but the emotion on the faces of these two women tells the entire story.

Street murder
(c.1940) Weegee does not shrink from the sight of blood or from the grim reality of death. This image hides nothing; a man has been gunned down on the street and Weegee has photographed the body, the blood and the gun. Another crime statistic becomes a haunting image of death, callously meted out.

114 **The Critic** *(1943)*
This is Weegee's
most celebrated
photograph. Two
ageing socialites
arriving at New
York's Metropolitan
Opera House, are
caught in the harsh
light of the photo-
grapher's flash gun.
Their smugness and
the almost caricatural
opulence of their
jewels contrast with
the pinched
expression and poor
clothes of the
woman who
watches them.

real name was Arthur Fellig, came to New York as the son of poor immigrant parents at the age of 10. In a 1965 interview he recalled his early years in America: 'I had very little schooling. . . . In them days you could quit school at 14, which I did, and went to work. One day, I saw an ad in the mail-order catalogue which I sent away for: a tintype camera, and I decided to go into photography.'

After working in various studios and undertaking a period of darkroom work at Acme Newspapers in about 1920, Weegee struck off on his own as a freelance news photographer. He soon earned a reputation as the first on the scene, the first with the picture and story and he impressed editors with the strength of his work. In the mid-1930s *Life* magazine presented a feature on him, but the true confirmation of his reputation came in 1945 with the publication of his first book, *The Naked City*, an anthology of his best work, and with an exhibition of his work at New York's Museum of Modern Art.

Regrettably, 1945 and the wide public recognition which came with book and exhibition marked the close of the most exciting phase in Weegee's career. He went to Hollywood, but was like a fish out of water, and subsequently indulged in a series of photo-distortion portraits of curiosity value rather than aesthetic merit.

The Weegee that will always be remembered is the pre-1945 Weegee, sleeping fully clothed, police radio by his pillow, ready to wake and respond to news of gangland killing or tenement fire; the unshaven, swearing, cigar-smoking Weegee whose car boot was his office and storeroom, complete with typewriter to crash out a story, spare film and flash bulbs. Photographic history has reserved a place for the Weegee who was friend of policemen and gangsters alike, who found sympathy for the losers, the freaks, the down-and-outs of the Bowery, the flotsam of society as well as all the ordinary folk whom he encountered in extraordinary situations. His greatest asset was his police radio and the exclusive privilege of having it installed in his car. His uncanny ability

to arrive on the scene, often even before the emergency services, is the explanation for his name, Weegee, derived from the ouija board, popularly regarded as a source of the psychic power of prediction.

In his work Weegee's concern was subject, not style, though his images have a directness, a frankness which is unmistakably his; and his beloved subject was people, caught off-guard. Two singularly memorable images well illustrate his approach. One, *The Critic*, perhaps his most famous photograph, shows two elegant society ladies arriving at New York's Metropolitan Opera House. While other photographers crowded the foyer to take the standard glamorous portraits, Weegee waited in the street: 'I like to get different shots and don't like to make the same shots the other dopes do. . . . I went into the street. . . . A nice Rolls Royce pulled up. . . . I waited till the occupants got out and snapped the picture. I couldn't see what I was snapping but could almost smell the smugness . . .' In the other photograph, a study of mother and daughter at a tenement fire, he has turned from the fire itself to concentrate on the emotion in the tortured Goyaesque faces of these two women whose relatives have perished.

Weegee kept no secrets. In *The Naked City* he explained his equipment and techniques. 'The only camera I use,' he wrote, 'is a 4 × 5in Speed Graphic with a Kodak Ektar Lens in a Supermatic shutter, all American made. The film I use is a Super Pancro Press Type B.' He continues to explain in great detail the stops he uses for different distances and that he always uses a flash bulb for his photographs, regardless of whether it is day or night. Weegee would never waste endless sheets of film where one timely exposure could suffice and his system of working to a fixed focus meant he was always ready for that timely shot. 'All over the world,' he said in the 1965 interview, 'people ask me: what is the secret of your formula? I just laugh; I have no formula, I'm just myself, take me or leave me. I don't put on an act, I don't try to make a good or bad impression. I'm just Weegee.'

115

lāzlō moholy-nagy

Hungarian/1895–1946

The illiterates of the future, said László Moholy-Nagy in 1928, will not be those who are ignorant of writing but those who are ignorant of photography. Of all the great photographers it was Moholy-Nagy who had the greatest hopes and ambitions for the medium. As someone who worshipped the modern world, he saw photography as its first great art form, an art form which could not have existed outside the modern world. He had no time for the 'clickers' or 'shutter snappers' as he called those photographers who were content to try and capture a moment in time. He accused them of trying to imitate painters. For Moholy-Nagy the photograph should be carefully considered and thought about. Above all, the camera should be itself and should not pretend to be an extension of the human eye.

Born in 1895 in Hungary, Moholy-Nagy went to Germany as a young man. During the 1920s, while he was working at the Bauhaus, Moholy-Nagy undertook an extensive series of photographic experiments. The Bauhaus preached the importance of materials exclusive to the modern world, the importance of technology and progress. Not only did Moholy-Nagy experiment with new materials, he also searched for new ways and directions in which to develop the photograph.

What made photography different from other art forms for Moholy-Nagy was that it dealt with light directly and not at second hand. Indeed, the photograph could be said to be made entirely of light, or rather the result of the action of light on light-sensitive paper. The 'reality' which other photographers searched for was illusory; only the light itself was real. A photograph is not made up of fragments of the visible world but of fragments of light. The camera, he said, 'is constructed on optical laws different from those of our eyes.' Photography has its own laws and effects and should not be judged on the laws of other media.

The photogram was Moholy-Nagy's key to a real awareness of what a photograph was. In these photograms he worked directly onto photographic paper, manipulating the light at first hand and doing away with the camera altogether. His first experiments took place at the beginning of the 1920s and he described them as primitive attempts. Using lenses and mirrors he passed light through assorted

"**Photography as a presentational art is not merely a copy of nature. This is proven by the fact that a 'good' photograph is a rare thing.**"

fluids like water, oil and acids, and cast it directly onto the sensitive plate. The self-portrait of Moholy-Nagy and his first wife, Lucia, was produced later when he began to experiment with daylight paper and watched how the sun would darken the paper around the forms he introduced between itself and the light source. The results were in fact a series of negatives. Moholy-Nagy liked the original brilliant white of the paper and the sharp contrasts he achieved with the deep blacks. He also enjoyed the 'differentiated play of light and shadow' which could be achieved by photography without a camera.

These photograms could in fact be developed but the photographer felt that the positives were spoiled by 'harsher, frequently ashy grey values.' The permeating light effects, the deep silhouettes which he created, tended to be flattened in the positives. In many ways these photograms are closer to the abstract paintings he was producing at the time than they are to traditional photography. But by treating the photographic paper as a clean sheet on which he could make sketches with light, he opened up the way for photographers and painters alike to work more directly with light.

Just as he continued experimenting with the photograms, so Moholy-Nagy found himself dissatisfied with 'realistic photography'. He began using multiple exposures and building up his images in layers. Even with his most traditional photography, produced as illustrations for such books as John Betjeman's *An Oxford University Chest* or Mary Benedetta's *The Streetmarkets of London*, he refused to be tied by photographic convention, by conventional perspectives and light effects, by conventional viewpoints and angles. There was no room in the modern world for Renaissance perspectives; the modern photographer could look down on the world from an aeroplane or a skyscraper. There was no need for the top of a building to disappear into the distance if the photographer could reach its roof by the lift.

Renaissance perspective was full of unattainable goals, symbolized by the speck on the horizon. For Moholy-Nagy there were no unattainable goals. Everything could be reached in stages.

His theory of simultaneous complexity, of the camera's ability to focus on everything at once, is best illustrated in his description of a shop window, much like the window of the Bexhill Pavilion, seen from a car: '. . . the windows of this car are transparent. Through them one sees a shop, which in turn has a transparent window. Inside, people, shoppers and traders. . . . in front of the shop walk passers-by. The traffic policeman stops a cyclist. One grasps all that in a single moment, because the panes are transparent and everything is happening in the line of sight. . . .' According to Moholy-Nagy the growth of the modern city and the technical developments which encouraged it, had sharpened the city dweller's senses but only the camera could really take in all this information at once.

As a painter and sculptor as well as a photographer, Moholy-Nagy, like MAN RAY, brought an awareness of current artistic activity to photography. The emphasis on movement in his work (he was one of the first to use long exposures so that a car's journey was preserved as an unbroken trail of light) was inherited from the Futurists. The combinations of metal and glass which could be found in modern architecture, like the Bexhill Pavilion, allowed him to see right into a building and out the other side, just as you could with his Constructivist sculpture. Yet he also pioneered the use of scientific photography which enabled him to look inside a beehive and photograph a drone clinging to a honeycomb.

Moholy-Nagy worked in so many styles at once, made so many different experiments, that he seemed to embody his own theory of simultaneous complexity. His photoplastics, or photomontages as he later called them, were yet another attempt at showing how the photograph could keep track with everything happening at once, his 'railway track of ideas.' Above all in these stirring, satirical collages he wanted to show how 'imitative' photography could be cut into little bits and then reassembled as something more purposeful and creative.

Photogram
(c.1930) Moholy-Nagy believed that photograms like this one reflected the 'unique nature of the photographic process' and were 'the key to photography', because they dealt so directly with light. Such photographs were produced by shining light onto ordinary objects, placed on sensitized paper and they allowed Moholy-Nagy to experiment with abstract designs.

man ray
American/1890–1976

"I paint what cannot be photographed, something from the imagination . . . I photograph the things I don't want to paint, things that are already in existence."

Man Ray was an artist who felt free to use both photography and painting as media to express his dreams and fantasies. Unwilling to restrict himself to one or the other, he often said 'I paint what cannot be photographed. I photograph what I do not wish to paint'. His willingness to break the rules and investigate darkroom accidents enabled Man Ray to develop several inventive photographic techniques.

Man Ray's origins are slightly mysterious. He was born in Philadelphia, Pennsylvania, possibly as Emmanuel Rudnitsky, in 1890 and at the age of seven decided to become an artist. After briefly studying architecture and engraving, he went to New York where he attended life drawing classes and began to frequent ALFRED STIEGLITZ's gallery '291' where he saw work by the most progressive painters and photographers of the day, responding to the new ideas with enthusiasm.

One of Man Ray's closest and most influential friendships began in New York, with the acquaintance of Marcel Duchamp, a young French artist whose Dadaist paintings and constructions were to be among the most controversial works of the twentieth century. The two men remained close friends and collaborators until Duchamp's death in 1968.

Man Ray began taking photographs because he needed pictures of his paintings for the press and collectors and, rather than pay a professional photographer, decided to do it himself, buying a camera and the filters necessary to translate colour into black and white. The results were excellent, and, as painting was not proving especially remunerative, Man Ray began to photograph other artists' work and portraits. His first subjects included his friends Duchamp, Edgar Varèse, Joseph Stella, Berenice Abbott and Djuna Barnes.

After mastering the camera, Man Ray discarded it temporarily, in order to try and combine painting with darkroom techniques. Cliche-verre was a process developed around 1820 and used by, among others, Corot, Delacroix, and Millet. The original technique consisted of a drawing being scratched onto a smoked glass plate with a needle. This was contact-printed onto a sheet of light-sensitized paper. The clear outlines of the drawing appeared

Kiki of Montmartre 119
(c.1928) A well-known singer and personality in her own right, Kiki was Man Ray's mistress and model for six years. She was the subject of many of Man Ray's most famous — or infamous — photographs including *Le Violon d'Ingres* (1924) in which he painted a violin's f-holes on her naked back. Kiki also starred in his experimental film *L'Etoile de Mer* (1926–1929).

Lee Miller *(1930)*
Man Ray's use of the Sabattier effect, in which light and dark tones are reversed, was inspired by an accident in his darkroom. He applied it most effectively in this portrait of Lee Miller. She was a young American who worked as Man Ray's assistant for several years and then went on to become a successful photographer herself.

120

black on the paper, and any number of prints could be made. Man Ray adapted this technique by exposing a glass plate negative to light and then scratching his drawing onto the negative's emulsion, sometimes drawing directly onto previously exposed negatives. His earliest Cliche-verres date from 1917, and he returned to the technique several times over the years.

With Duchamp's help, Man Ray left New York in 1921 and settled in Paris. He aligned himself with the Dada and Surrealist movements and took part in numerous exhibitions and publishing ventures. In order to support himself he began to take on commercial assignments, becoming a successful, highly paid portraitist, and also doing some fashion work. Several photographers who were to become well-known worked as Man Ray's assistants including Berenice Abbott, BILL BRANDT, and Lee Miller. His sitters came primarily from the art world and included painters and sculptors like Picasso, Léger, Braque, Derain, Matisse, Gris, Brancusi, and Giacometti; and writers and poets such as Virginia Woolf, T S Eliot, Joyce, and Hemingway.

Although Man Ray usually controlled and planned the portrait sittings according to his vision of the individual involved, he occasionally found it difficult to dictate to his subject. One such case was a session with the Marchesa Casati, a formidable and imperiously aristocratic poetess. Sum-

Hans Arp *(c.1935)*
This portrait, with its strong use of light and shadow, is a typical example of the many that Man Ray made of influential artists and friends. Man Ray came into contact with the French sculptor through his associations with the Dada movement

moned to her hotel on the Place Vendôme, Man Ray set up his equipment and immediately blew all the fuses. Having to work only with the available dim lighting, he asked the Marchesa to hold still for the long exposures necessary. She failed to do so, and her portraits, which Man Ray considered a total failure, were blurred. Demanding to see them, the Marchesa declared that one of the photographs, in which she appeared to have three pairs of eyes, was a portrayal of her soul and ordered dozens of prints.

In 1921 Man Ray made another fruitful discovery. While developing some fashion photographs for the designer Paul Poiret, he accidentally put an unexposed sheet of paper into the developer. After several minutes no image had appeared, and, placing a funnel, measuring jug, and thermometer on the wet paper, Man Ray turned on the light. An image of the silhouettes of the objects appeared against a dark ground, slightly distorted due to the varying diffusive qualities of the light through the objects. Man Ray achieved dimension and tone with multiple exposures and by varying the distance of the object from the paper.

Excited by the possibilities of his new discovery, Man Ray began to create his 'Rayographs', as he later called them, using all sorts of different objects. Bits of paper, nails, a gun, gyroscopes, parts of the human body — all were subject to his whims; and as Man Ray said, 'Everything can be transformed by light. Light is an instrument as subtle as the brush.' The Surrealists were greatly excited by his 'Rayographs', and suggested that he publish some of them in a portfolio. Thus in 1922, *Les Champs Délicieux* was published in book form.

Another darkroom accident prompted Man Ray's use of the Sabattier effect, or solarization, which is achieved by re-exposure of a negative or print during development. The re-exposure causes a reversal of light and dark tones, and creates a dark line around the subject's contours. Man Ray used the technique brilliantly but sparingly in portraits, nudes, and still-life studies, producing subtle variations in tonality.

Man Ray left Paris in 1940, with the coming of the German Occupation, and went to Hollywood, California, where he remained until 1951. He then returned to Paris where he lived until his death in 1976. Technique was of little interest to Man Ray, what counted was the end result. A sense of play, of magic, and a fascination with visual perception characterizes all of his work, but was most fully realized in his 'Rayographs' and portraits.

andré kertész

Austrian/born 1894

"I believe that you should be a perfect technician in order to express yourself as you wish."

Born in Budapest in 1894, André Kertész bought an inexpensive box camera with his first wage packet which he earned as a stock exchange accountant. One of the earliest plates Kertész exposed was the photograph *A Young Man Sleeping*, 1912, which was already the work of a master. The upright format, the closeness to the subject, the precise delineation of the shadowy background and the wry response to the situation all seem too per-fectly conceived to be the work of a novice. But then Kertész had, by his own account, been imagining pictures for years before he could afford a camera to take them with; when he finally acquired one, he knew little about technique, but a great deal about his intended subject matter. Years later he was to describe the art of photography as 'little happenings' and no photographer has perceived or recorded more persuasively.

A Young Man Sleeping
(bromide print/ 1912) This is one of Kertész's earliest pictures, taken when he was only 18. From the news-papers surrounding the young man, he is obviously in a Budapest café which encouraged its customers to sit and relax, even when their coffee was finished. But this relaxation has not prevented the photographer from composing the picture very rigorously, as he was to do through-out his career. Here he uses a precise 'X' symmetry.

Distortion No 6
(bromide print/ 1933) In 1933, the publisher of a Paris 'girly' magazine, *Le Sourire*, approached Kertész (through a third party) to take pictures for it. He took about 100 photographs of nude women reflected in a fairground distorting mirror, but after a month or so he felt he had exhausted the potential of the idea. A plan to publish a book of the pictures fell through. Kertész's *Distortions* finally appeared in New York in 1976.

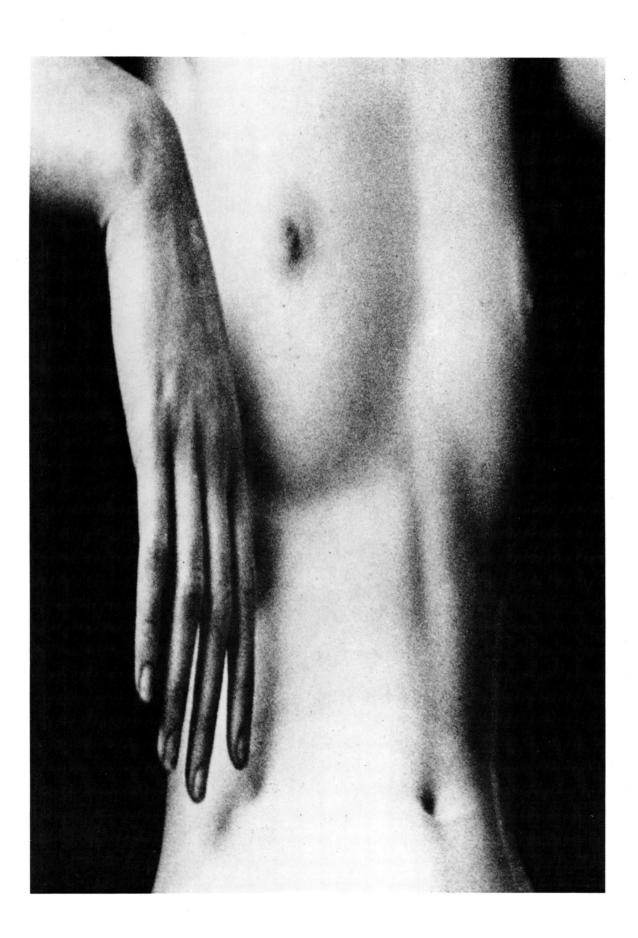

123

124

Underwater Swimmer *(bromide print/1917)* Taken in the historic Danube resort of Esztergom (where Kertész was convalescing from a bullet wound which left him partly paralyzed for nearly a year), this influential photograph shows Kertész's unique way of seeing. The strange shapes made by the play of light on the water and the swimmer's body derive, not from his imagination, but his observation.

125

126

Kertész enlisted at the outbreak of the First World War, taking his camera with him. His first photograph to receive public recognition was a self-portrait of a 21 year old soldier scrubbing himself clean of the fleas which infested him. This won a small prize in an amateur photography competition. Kertész was quite seriously wounded, and for almost a year was convalescent, spending much of his enforced rest photographing his fellow patients and the people who lived round the hospital. One photograph was taken while sitting on the steps of a swimming pool, and resulted in a pioneering and influential picture in which the apparently headless form of a diver snakes through the rippled water. Looking at the expressive distortions of the human form favoured by so many contemporary painters, sculptors and photographers, it is difficult to believe they have not been influenced by *Underwater Swimmer*, 1917. Kertész experimented with distortions again, notably in a series of nudes taken for the Paris magazine *Le Sourire* in 1933, but was never able to recapture the unforced naturalism of the original photograph.

During and after the war, Kertész's photographs continued to attract modest attention. In 1925, a magazine used one of his views of the old city of Buda on its cover and this success, together with his dissatisfaction with an office career and Hungary's increasingly difficult political situation, led Kertész to leave for Paris. He made his home in Montparnasse and met many other artists including Brancusi, Chagall, Léger and Mondrian. Kertész photographed the artists and their studios, but was more interested in candid street scenes, especially after he bought his first Leica in 1928.

In the artistic atmosphere of perhaps the only city where he has ever felt truly at home, with a camera that seemed purpose-built for his kind of unobtrusive documentary photography, Kertész produced many of his finest works. One photograph, *Meudon*, 1928, illustrates three of his talents. Firstly, Kertész's ability to capture the feeling of movement by calculating — or knowing instinctively — the exact exposure to use, producing not harsh sharpness nor obvious blurring, but an impressionistic image. Another is Kertész's ability to encompass several scenes and subjects in one coherent picture through a mastery of composition and focus which again springs more from instinct than the following of rules. The third is patience; patience to wait for all the elements of the picture to come together at exactly the right moment.

Kertész's 'exact moment' is not quite CARTIER-BRESSON's 'decisive' one. For Kertész, instinct and emotion are always foremost, whereas Cartier-Bresson depends more on calculation and planning. But Cartier-Bresson acknowledges his debt to the older photographer, 'my poetic wellspring'. Another photographer in Paris at the time — along with Robert Capa, MAN RAY, Berenice Abbott and BILL BRANDT — who was strongly influenced by Kertész was his fellow Hungarian BRASSAI. Indeed, Brassaï, a painter and sculptor, had never taken a photograph until Kertész showed him how, and lent him a camera. Brassaï was to continue Kertész's mastery of city night photography.

In 1927, Kertész was given his first one-man exhibition at the Au Sacré du Printemps gallery. By now his work was appearing regularly in all the German illustrated news magazines, as well as in the Paris journal *Vu*. He was included in Paris's first 'Independent Salon of Photography' exhibition in 1928; Essen's 'Contemporary Photography' and Stuttgart's 'Film und Foto', the first major exhibition of modern 'neo-realist' photography, a year later. German museums purchased his work, German galleries showed it, and in 1932 Kertész exhibited in Brussels and New York. His international reputation as an artist-photographer was second to none.

In 1936, Kertész left Europe to take up a year's contract with a New York picture agency which turned out to be a mistake. His subtle, European taste was not that of American editors, and the scale and inhumanity of New York was frighteningly alien to him. But as the First World War had trapped him in a hospital, the Second World War forced him away from Europe. After the war, Kertész was able to earn a good living as a contract photographer for the magazine publisher Condé Nast, but his personal photographs reveal an increasing fascination with the abstract patterns created by buildings — especially when photographed from his twelfth floor apartment which overlooked Washington Square — and a decreasing interest in people. Evidently, there were few people Kertész was prepared to trust and when his wife died — perhaps the only one he really trusted — his creativity, too, died for a time.

However, Kertész has never stopped making photographs and his latest coloured still-lifes taken with a Polaroid camera, reveal that he has not lost his ability to surprise, nor to show things the normal eye might well see but usually fails to perceive.

Washington Square *(bromide print/1954)* For many years, Kertész has lived in an apartment in New York's Greenwich Village. He and his wife Elizabeth bought this partly because of the angle of vision it gave on the constantly shifting panorama of people, events and seasons in Washington Square, 12 floors below. Kertész photographs these with a 'zoom' lens, which he has favoured ever since he first acquired a primitive one in Paris in 1929.

127

walker evans

American/1903–1975

Walker Evans was an artist with great interest in the appearances of everyday life. His work is characterized by an attraction to the ordinary, often depicted in an unadorned, seemingly artless manner. Simple as they appear, Evans' photographs are skilful evocations of American life.

Born in 1903 in St Louis, Missouri, Evans was educated at a variety of private schools, and spent one year at Williams College, Williamstown, Massachusetts. In 1922 he went to Paris with the ambition of becoming a writer, but a year later was back in New York, penniless and disillusioned. He took a job as a stock clerk with a Wall Street brokerage firm, but found it unfulfilling and soon left. It was around this time that Evans began to consider photography as a possible career, and as an art which he might both master and use creatively.

Evans' first photographs were made in 1928 in New York, using a camera which produced $2\frac{1}{4} \times 4\frac{1}{4}$in negatives. From the start, he worked in a consciously 'unartistic' manner. Unlike the pictorialists, whose desire to make 'artistic' photographs resulted in painterly images, and unlike STIEGLITZ, who photographed common scenes and imbued them with dramatic emotion, Evans' intention was to make straightforward representations of life, with no imprint of personal style; he believed in the eloquence of his subject matter.

Friendships with artists and writers like Ben Shahn and Hart Crane kept Evans in touch with current trends and progressive ideas, and with an enlightened, knowledgable eye he set out to photograph the big cities and small towns of the United States. In 1931, accompanied by Lincoln Kirstein, a young intellectual who played an important role in the development of American cultural life, Evans photographed Victorian houses in Boston, Massachusetts. He used an old-fashioned view camera which used 6 × 8in glass plate negatives. In his diary, Kirstein wrote of Evans' painstaking approach and high standards, and his willingness to wait for hours on end for perfect lighting conditions. Although the results of the expedition far exceeded Kirstein's expec-

128

"How do I go about composing and taking a picture? Well again, more or less instinctively. That's a self-taught procedure. I don't do it very consciously. In fact, I don't think you should be very conscious in photography of classic rules of graphic composition."

tations, Evans was less than satisfied. In 1931 Evans became involved in advertising photographs, but like stockbroking, this was not a great success.

Evans' next assignment in 1932 was to illustrate Carleton Beals' *The Crime of Cuba*. The resulting photographs are a mixture of portraiture, architectural details, street views, and interesting oddments. Evans photographed dock workers, prostitutes, newsboys, sugar cane farms, local cinemas, and religious ornaments. He made elegant, controlled images which chronicled the changing face of Cuban life, and foreshadowed the breadth and diversity of means he was to employ two years later in the American South.

The period from 1935 to 1936 was a time of great creativity for Evans. During these 18 months he worked as a Farm Security Administration (FSA) photographer, and his vision and technique came together, producing many images of lasting strength. The FSA was a Federal programme set up to document the plight of rural Americans during the Depression. Directed by Roy Stryker, the FSA assigned photographers to cover certain geographic areas. Some of the better-known photographers employed by the scheme included Dorothea Lange, Russell Lee, and Arthur Rothstein. Travelling back and forth across Alabama, Mississippi, Georgia, South Carolina and Louisiana, Evans gave as much attention to peeling vaudeville signs as to country churches, and succeeded in capturing the subtle complexities of a time of poverty and depression.

In 1936 Evans and James Agee spent six weeks in Alabama with a tenant farm family. The Burroughs were poor, their children wore ragged clothes, and they worked endless hours for little recompense. Evans photographed them with both compassion and detachment; by showing their lives simply and directly, and by avoiding

overt comment, he was able to create portraits of great dignity, which never condescend. With an accompanying text by Agee, these pictures were later published as the book *Let Us Now Praise Famous Men*, 1941.

In 1938 Evans had the first one-man photographic exhibition ever held at the Museum of Modern Art in New York. To accompany the show, the Museum published a book of the images exhibited. *American Photographs* was a composite portrait of life at that time; urban landscapes, portraits, and interiors all added up to an uncompromisingly bleak view of the United States.

In complete contrast to his use of the view camera — which afforded the photographer great flexibility in the adjustment of focus and perspective, but was conspicuous, slow, and unwieldy — in 1938 Evans began to use a small 35mm Contax camera in a radically different way. He began to photograph the New York City subways, concealing the camera beneath his coat. With no control over framing and composition, Evans was forced to concentrate on the faces and gestures of his fellow travellers. The series of photographs were published in book form in 1966 as *Many Are Called*.

From 1945 to 1965, Evans was a writer and photographer for *Fortune* magazine. In many cases, Evans both conceived and carried out ideas which were of specific personal interest. His love of American vernacular architecture is evident in the story he did on the old woollen mills of New England, which were once the basis of American industry. He also used old office interiors, hotels, and other less antique subjects like the trucking industry; and explored his interest in spontaneous, unpremeditated photography in two articles on the streets of Chicago and Detroit.

In addition to his photographic work, Evans served as mentor and advisor to a younger generation of photographers, among them ROBERT FRANK, who worked with him on a *Fortune* article, *Beauties of the Common Tool*. From 1965 until his death in 1975, Evans was Professor of Photography at Yale University.

Fireplace and objects in a bedroom of Floyd Burroughs' home, Hale County, Alabama *(1936)* Evans, like many of his contemporaries, believed that people make art in the normal course of events, whether they are aware of being artists or not. He found evidence for this view in the shrines which people in the rural South apparently contrived for themselves in their kitchens and living rooms. He also had a taste for symmetrical arrangements like this, because they invite comparisons between objects between one side of the image and the other. Thus the viewer is invited to note minute differences between superficially similar everyday objects.

cecil beaton

British/1904–1980

**"Steichen influenced me in a particular way:
he forced me to use a different camera, an
enormous camera, not my little Kodak."**

Born into a privileged milieu, Cecil Beaton was well-placed to record the styles, fashions, and concerns of an influential era. Best known as a flattering portraitist of the upper classes, Beaton actually worked in many styles, often pursuing subjects which would seem to have little appeal for one so obsessed with fashion.

Beaton's early life and childhood was traditionally comfortable. He has traced his interest in photography to an early infatuation with Lily Elsie, an actress whose picture-postcard likeness he had seen when he was a mere three years old. The magic of a medium which could produce such a beautiful image appealed to him, and at the age of 11 Beaton was given his

first camera. Aided by his sister's nurse he began to make romantic pictorial images which were influenced by fashion photographs and contemporary aesthetic conventions.

Beaton's favourite subjects were his two sisters, Nancy and Baba. In his pursuit of fantasy, elegance, and sophistication, Beaton utilized all sorts of household objects. He swathed his patient sitters in yards of lace, sheets, and oriental carpets, strewed flowers everywhere, and painted special backdrops to enhance the period settings. Although he could work for hours devising complicated costumes and environments, Beaton was confounded by the technical aspects of photography, and

130 **Edith Sitwell**
(1962) Among Beaton's favourite friends and collaborators were Edith Sitwell and her brothers. They were champions of his photography and the eccentric poetess, clad in flowing robes, would often pose in exotic settings for Beaton's camera. This portrait, concentrating on her unusual profile and her fingers heavily bedecked with rings, conveys her forceful personality.

Nancy Beaton
(1926) A fantasia rather than a true portrait, this picture of Beaton's sister is typical of much of his early work. Along with a faintly absurd head-dress, much use has been made of crinkled cellophane. Beaton took the portrait with a primitive Kodak box camera which he often used throughout his career and from which he often coaxed astonishing results.

for much of his career he used only a simple box camera.

In 1922, at his father's urging, Beaton entered Cambridge University. Unconventionality and flamboyant aestheticism were the prevailing modes of the day, and Beaton entered in with enthusiasm. Never a scholar, his main interest was in drama, and his photographs of Cambridge thespians brought Beaton to the attention of the editor of British *Vogue*. In 1924 a portrait of his friend George Rylands, attired for the title role of *The Duchess of Malfi*, appeared in the magazine and was Beaton's first published work.

After leaving Cambridge and trying for several months to support himself with photographic commissions, Beaton was forced to take an accounting job in his father's timber company. Unsuited to business, Beaton nevertheless tried to satisfy his father's desires while pursuing a photographic career, but finally gave up in 1926 and opened a portrait studio in his family's house in London's Sussex Gardens. Beaton was quickly deluged with commissions, and his flattering yet non-traditional approach became the rage.

The unconventional use of settings and props which Beaton had employed in the first early portraits of his sisters climaxed in the pictures he made of debutantes and celebrities. The special qualities of each sitter, be they beautiful or eccentric, were highlighted by the use of appropriate backdrops and points of view. Some of these portraits seem dated and unconvincing to the contemporary eye, but at the time they were a decisive break with the static conventions of the past.

Beaton's ability and desire to flatter knew no bounds. Truth in a portrait was purely subjective, and beauty could be conjured up with a re-touching brush. Unsightly bulges and mottled complexions disappeared instantly, and society matrons, with the help of Beaton's charitable art, were once again svelte and young.

In 1929, Beaton was finally on the verge of fulfilling his dreams of fame, success, and glamour. He was offered the opportunity to work for American *Vogue*, and in November of that year left for New York. After a disappointing start, Beaton portraits of luminaries such as Fred Astaire and Gertrude Lawrence began to appear in the pages of *Vogue*, and he was soon under contract to the publisher.

The years that followed found Beaton playing the role of court photographer to the 'smart set'. He photographed in Hollywood, where he met Greta Garbo, the great love of his life, and travelled wherever and whenever he could. When released from the confines of the studio, Beaton worked in a more instinctive manner,

choosing to record offbeat, sometimes surreal subjects. Beaton was summoned to France in 1937 to photograph Edward VIII and Mrs Simpson on their wedding day and two years later, was called upon to photograph Queen Elizabeth, the wife of King George VI. Throughout the years he continued to be the favoured portraitist to the British royal family.

Until his association with Condé Nast, Beaton had been creating his amazing portraits with a battered Kodak pocket camera. This allowed for spontaneity, was light and easy to use, but often unreliable. In addition, only small portions of these negatives could be used, and prints were often out of focus. Beaton was finally forced to use a more cumbersome and heavy 8 × 10in camera, which forced him to work in a more thoughtful way and gave greater clarity. He was now able to see exactly what the picture would look like on the ground glass camera back, and corrections in composition and perspective were much more easily made. Thus Beaton was able to make photographs which were better organized and less a product of chance.

The Second World War put an end to the glamorous world which Beaton and his friends had constructed. In 1940, having spent six weeks in New York on commercial assignments, Beaton returned to England, where he was appointed photographer for the Ministry of Information. He was instructed to take pictures of London during the bombings, which were used for propaganda purposes both in Britain and abroad. During the war Beaton also photographed military operations in England, Egypt, and the Far East.

After the war, Beaton returned to commercial photography as a means of support. Working for *Vogue* in 1946 he created a series of fashion photographs entitled 'The New Reality'. The pictures were anything but realistic, showing chic models engaged in mundane tasks. Although the series was a great success, within several years Beaton found himself and his work out of date. Highly artificial stylizations were no longer in demand, and fashion editors disdained his tableaux. He returned to his first love, the theatre, and won awards for his sets and costumes for the films *Gigi* and *My Fair Lady*.

In the 1960s and 1970s, Beaton once again aligned himself with youth and vitality, photographing friends like pop-star Mick Jagger and artist David Hockney. He occasionally took on commercial assignments until he suffered an incapacitating stroke in 1974. A partial recovery allowed him to begin work again, and just before his death in 1980 he photographed the Paris collections for French *Vogue*.

Hat check girl
(1946) After serving as a photographer for the Ministry of Information during the war, Beaton returned to the United States to continue working for *Vogue*. This image was one in the series in which he photographed bored, elegant mannequins in highly artificial sets. Beaton was able to create slickly controlled, commercial images which were ironically devoid of reality.

132

133

erwin blumenfeld

German-born American/ 1897–1969

"He is a master technician who creates his own camera magic by translating and embellishing what the lens sees."
(Bettina Ballard, Vogue editor)

Erwin Blumenfeld's life has been described as a twentieth-century odyssey, 'remarkable, strange and violent. He was a German Jew, and his cynicism, morbidness, and traumatized imagination, fed by the unstable years he spent in Europe, found a highly personal and expressive outlet in photography. For Blumenfeld, photography became the cathartic medium for his urgent need to explore complex and obsessive themes and visions. It opened up creative possibilities for which his exploration of graphic techniques, including collage, had served as a stimulus.

For Blumenfeld, photography was also to become the key to material success. When he finally settled in New York in the 1940s – the 'promised land' for so many rootless exiles – Blumenfeld became a willing cog in the machine of commercial photography. His success in this field altered the direction of his work, softening

134

Nude *(1943)* In this complex multiple exposure colour image Blumenfeld has achieved an effect which might have been described as psychedelic 25 years later. The multiple exposure creates an illusion of movement and also allows the viewer to perceive the naked figure in the round.

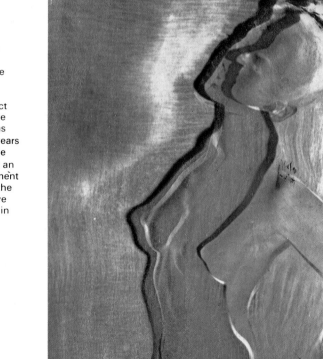

Wet veil II *(1937)* This image was first published in the pages of the avant-garde art journal, *Verve*. A technically straightforward photograph, it is nonetheless a clever one in which a sense of mystery is created by the photographer's idea of draping a damp muslin sheet over his model. Her nakedness is half-revealed and, perhaps more significantly, half-concealed.

its aggressive edge without diluting his creativity or his individuality.

Erwin Blumenfeld was born in Berlin in 1897. During the First World War, in 1916, he became a reluctant recruit in the German ambulance corps and in 1918, at the first opportunity, he fled to Holland. Here he made contact with members of the Dutch Dada movement, who were to shape and influence him artistically. After his marriage in 1921 to Lena Citroën he became a shopkeeper, with a leather-goods business in Amsterdam. Photography was for the moment still an amateur pre-occupation for Blumenfeld, but the collapse of his business in 1935 prompted his move to Paris where he devoted himself to creative photography. In March 1936 he had his first exhibition.

Blumenfeld's early days in Paris were creative but difficult; non-commercial photography not being a viable way to pay the rent. However, in Paris, he did discover it was possible to earn a reputation, and the strength and individuality of his work soon won the attention of art directors and editors. Before long, commercial commissions were easing the practical difficulties of Blumenfeld's life in Paris.

The intellectual and cultural life of Paris was as rich in these years as Blumenfeld's native Germany was stifled, and among the stars in the Parisian galaxy were many other expatriates. Their work, together with that of the French avant-garde, was published in a variety of inspired art journals; notable among these were *Vu*, *Minotaure* and *Verve*. It was in the first issue of *Verve* in 1937 that Blumenfeld published his first portfolio, 17 photographs which shared space with works by MAN RAY, Dora Maar, Florence Henri, BRASSAI and CARTIER-BRESSON among others. In the following year came Blumenfeld's first commissions from *Vogue* magazine, and in 1939 *Harper's Bazaar* vied with their rival for the services of this powerful new talent.

Returning to France from his first exploratory trip to New York, Blumenfeld was trapped by the circumstances of the Second World War and suffered a period of internment. In 1941 he emigrated to the United States, which was to become his final adopted homeland. After sharing a studio with the inspired and influential fashion photographer Martin Munkasci, in 1943 Blumenfeld set up his own studio in New York. He was soon to rank amongst the most successful commercial freelancers, with a prolific output of fashion and advertising work, including innumerable stylish covers for many magazines, most notably *Vogue*.

Changing styles and the advent of a new generation of photographers with new approaches and ideas gradually eclipsed Blumenfeld's reputation. The late 1950s found him pouring his energies into a remarkable autobiography, published posthumously in 1975 under the title *Jadis et Daguerre*. Blumenfeld died of a heart attack on 4 July 1969.

The themes which concerned Blumenfeld and which became the subject matter of his creative work were universal, although his viewpoint was often unconventional and the techniques he used in the realization of his images often innovative and personalized. Woman — her eroticism, substance and essence, woman as symbol, woman as mystery — was Blumenfeld's obsession. He also explored the symbolism of death and decay; the passing of time; and was equally fascinated by the timeless mysteries of the inner character and the intangible soul of the inanimate. Such concerns formed the very basis of Blumenfeld's work and provided the element of inspiration which lifted his commercial work above the mundane.

The common thread which ran through Blumenfeld's studio effects, his approach to picture taking, and his darkroom techniques, was the need to counteract the inherent 'literalness' of the photographic image and his methods thus infused a poetic ambiguity into his images. In framing an image, he would often use close-ups to give a seemingly abstract quality to his subject, or use a frame within a frame — be it a window, venetian blind or openwork architectural detail — to create a confusion of planes and an isolation of detail. At other times he would impose an intermediary layer between himself and his subject; his *Wet Veil* of 1937 is a justly celebrated exercise in this technique. The half-revealed figure is shrouded in mystery, the wet muslin responsible for the metamorphosis of a simple naked model into a symbol of woman.

The use of mirrors, double or multiple exposures or printings gave Blumenfeld's images the added dimension sought by the Cubists through their graphic explanations of substance. The grids and patterns of superimposed textures and the patterns created by deliberate reticulation of the negative were further means exploited by Blumenfeld to escape the harsh realism of the lens in his pursuit of the essence of his subjects. He also used the then popular darkroom technique of solarization, as well as the technique of printing only selected details from a negative, to isolate particular features of the subject.

In his colour work, Blumenfeld was as individualistic as when working in black and white. His greatest talent was his ability to show restraint, allowing a vivid touch of colour to enliven an almost monochromatic image, a technique put regularly to good effect in a succession of striking *Vogue* covers.

For Erwin Blumenfeld, technique was a major element of photographic image-making. Bettina Ballard, a *Vogue* editor with whom he worked, wrote in 1960 that, 'Blumenfeld's pictures are triumphs of the darkroom. He . . . is a master technician who creates his own camera magic by translating and embellishing what the lens sees.'

Doe-eyed Beauty *(1950)* This stylish study of sophisticated beauty Jean Patchett was used as the basis for a memorable *Vogue* cover in which a striking effect was achieved.

henri cartier-bresson

French/born 1908

" We are passive onlookers in a world that moves perpetually. Our only moment of creation is that 1/125 of a second when the shutter clicks. "

Henri Cartier-Bresson was born in Chantaloup, France in 1908, originally studying painting until becoming seriously interested in photography in 1930. After travelling until 1936, Cartier-Bresson returned to France and became involved in film-making, making, among others, a documentary on the Spanish Civil War. From the late 1940s, the name Henri Cartier-Bresson has been virtually synonymous with photography. His reputation was fully confirmed in 1952 with the publication of his first major book *Images à la Sauvette*, (*The Decisive Moment*). In 1955 *Les Européens* (*The Europeans*) was published, and in the same year his photographs were exhibited at the Pavillon de Marsan at the Louvre. Shortly afterwards came books on Moscow (*Moscou*, 1955) and China *D'Une Chine à l'Autre*, 1955 (*Photographs of China*). During the 1960s he was revered by a younger generation of photographers. JOEL MEYEROWITZ, in the introduction to his book *Cape Light* (1978), recalls spotting him for the first time at a St Patrick's Day parade in New York City in 1963: 'I saw a man jumping around, bobbing and weaving, twisting and turning, dancing; he was just terrific . . . I was shaking; I was *shaking*! I couldn't believe that we would have the luck to meet the master in this situation.'

Cartier-Bresson is a 'human interest' photographer, and was the first to give a full account of his practice. In his foreword to *The Decisive Moment*, he strongly emphasizes the importance of being in the middle of things, absorbed by events. He virtually disclaims responsibility and suggests that it is the events themselves which provoke 'the organic rhythm of forms'. According to Cartier-Bresson, a photographer able to work in unison with this rhythm will find a moment when form fits its subject matter. In this respect he is following Surrealist procedures; they too believed that the artist should be absorbed in the 'creative process' and carried along by the organic rhythm of forms.

At the same time, 'the decisive moment' had a prototype in photography itself. During the late 1920s, manoeuverable lightweight cameras such as the Ermanox and the Leica, which Cartier-Bresson uses, made possible a new and dynamic type of

Place de l'Europe *(1932)* A sprightly figure leaping lightly on a poster mocks this bulky figure about to lurch into the wet. In the 1930s, and after, French photographers believed that it was possible to have insights into the hopes and fears of other people, as well as into the conduct of their daily life. Henri Cartier-Bresson delights in insight. Here, he shows that the marooned man has done his best, even if hopelessly, to escape the flood.

sports photography. Reporters scrutinized sporting events for 'the psychological moment' and watched for 'effort at the moment of maximum intensity'. These phrases are taken from the sports pages of *Vu* magazine, the French illustrated weekly paper founded in 1928, in which Cartier-Bresson published his first pictures. He took the idea of 'the psychological moment' and applied it to society at large, and, in so doing wrought a great trans-

formation in tne role of the photojournalist, who formerly had been expected to
work according to well-established pictorial stereotypes. Surrealist beliefs, lightweight cameras and new ideas in sports
photography all helped to liberate photo-
journalism.

In addition, Cartier-Bresson had the
example of ANDRE KERTESZ. Kertész had
moved to Paris from Budapest in 1925
and became one of the principal pho-

**The banks of the
Loing (Seine et
Marne)** *(c.1965)*
Photographers did
not invent a modern
idea of Frenchness
all by themselves.
They were part of a
movement which
included film-
makers René Clair
and Jean Renoir.

Yet they were
enormously
important in
establishing an idea
of the French as a
fundamentally
traditional people,
under their modern
trappings. Cartier-
Bresson's city men
attend absorbed to
their angling, despite

the imminent
ruination of a pair of
shoes.

Château Biron, Dordogne *(1969)* Europeans who survived the Second World War returned with relief to their traditional ways. French photography after 1945 shows an ancient land, imbued with tradition and peopled by timeless cultivators. This picture of Old France is one of the most complete images within the traditional mode; it shows France conceived as it had been in the fifteenth century by the illustrator of the 'Très Riches Heures of the Duc de Berry' — as a land of seasonal labour and settled society.

Matisse à Saint-Jean-Cap-Ferrat *(1952)* French photographers were appreciative of French painters. They understood what they were up to. As in so many of Henri Matisse's own paintings a mirror doubles the image. It holds a picture of the vase just as the painter himself recreates the curve of the bowl and the curve of a buttock with a gesture of his hand. Picasso, Bonnard, Braque and Matisse were much photographed in the years of peace after 1945 — they represented civilization saved.

tographers for *Vu* magazine to which he brought irreverence and a taste for the peripheral pleasures of life. Cartier-Bresson, who acknowledges the influence of Kertész on him, also brings the peripheral into the foreground; he works with the audience rather than with the parade, and watches for incidental details which might be symptomatic of some greater cultural whole.

Moreover, Cartier-Bresson comes from a society which attaches importance to psychological realism in its art, and thinks in terms of insight into others. For example, the stories of the French realist writers like Guy de Maupassant show people as knowable, as possessors of secrets, aspirations and cherished habits. Cartier-Bresson's photographs are elaborate essays on this same understanding but in a different and newer medium. Some of his greatest pictures are extraordinarily revealing. One such, published wherever the photography of Cartier-Bresson is mentioned, is *Sunday on the banks of the Marne*, 1938. Two family groups picnic on the shelving bank of the river. They look towards the water and their elegant boat and, with their faces hidden, give nothing away. Yet the picture is redolent with clues. Costume, position and gesture all point to a rich story. The foreground figure, in a dark hat and braces on a warm, summer's day, is an embodiment of prudence, positioned towards the crest of the bank, safe from spillage and inconvenience.

Cartier-Bresson relishes such signs of prudence. His people manage as best they can, keeping their wits about them and avoiding difficult situations. They defer to uniforms and to Party bosses and, even when in the tender throes of love, make sure that lighted cigarettes are kept out of harm's way.

One of the most influential of all photographers, Cartier-Bresson has never been outdone; no other photographer offers a comparable degree of insight into the lives of others. Remarkably, in a profession where careers are often short and brilliant, he has maintained a consistent level of achievement for over half a century. Clearly, human prudence is endlessly fascinating, and the minor pleasures of life countless.

Cartier-Bresson's greatest achievement might well have been the creation, or at least establishment, of a particular image of France as a land peopled by singular personalities: crabbed and lined peasants, shrewd *bourgeoisie*, vivid children. During 1936 and 1937 he worked as an assistant director to the film-maker Jean Renoir in the making of *Une Partie de Campagne* and *La Règle du Jeu* (*Rules of the Game*). Renoir's vision of France, and of human nature, was in many ways very like Cartier-Bresson's.

Perhaps more importantly, Cartier-Bresson gave Europeans suffering from the ruination of war a rich vision of what settled domesticity could be like. His France is a land of milk and honey, vines and orderly farms. Moreover, it is a strongly traditional land in which café life flourishes and the business of small towns proceeds in a classical and undisturbed environment. Cartier-Bresson brought the same message from abroad, finding signs of worship, devotion and tradition wherever he went, be it China, India, Indonesia or the Soviet Union. Overseas, however, he had less access to psychological and social truths. In the East he found great formal beauty, but few of the intensely revealing signs which mark his French pictures.

Taking his cue from Kertész in the early 1930s, Cartier-Bresson became France's greatest photojournalist. Britain, leaning towards a more theatrical idea of social life, produced no major photojournalist in this vein; nor did the United States, where a taste for activism and a romantic regard for the primacy of feeling led to an altogether different type of photoreportage. The peers of Cartier-Bresson are French photographers who learned from his example: Willy Ronis, one of photography's most benign artists, who worked emphatically to project a picture of domestic tranquillity; Robert Doisneau, responsible for a wealth of genial insights into the many-sided French. But it is Cartier-Bresson above all who recalled the intense pleasures to be found along the way: either in daily life or after the parade's gone by.

brassai

Gyula Halász/French/born 1899

"I want my subject to be as fully conscious as possible – fully aware that he is taking part in an artistic event, an act."

Exciting, charged with creative energy, a place which draws artists from all over the world, Paris has served as inspiration for many great talents. Brassaï, born Gyula Halász in Transylvania, Hungary, has been described as the 'eye of Paris' by his friend Henry Miller, having adopted the city as his own in 1923. After studying painting in Budapest and Berlin, at the age of 24 Brassaï went to Paris where he quickly established close friendships with other artists and writers. Fearing that his given name was too difficult to pronounce, he changed his name to Brassaï, in honour of his native town Brasso, when his first essays were published.

Brassaï's early years in Paris were unconventional. Fascinated by city life after dark, he spent the days sleeping and walked all night; he wandered over all of Paris, savouring the hidden areas, drawn to an unfamiliar way of life which

Picasso, rue de la Boetie *(1932)* Like Brassai, Picasso was inspired by Paris and he lived and worked there for many years. Here, the photographer has captured Picasso in an informal pose, with a cigarette in his hand. The lighting focuses the viewer's attention onto his face rather than onto the cluttered background of paints and palettes.

Prostitute playing Russian billiards *(c.1932)* Brassai used a camera on a tripod and artificial lighting to take this photograph of a prostitute in a bar on the Boulevard Rochechouart in Montmartre. Her bold glance and open-faced acknowledgement of the photographer's presence exemplifies the rapport which Brassai achieved with his subjects.

144 flourished only under cover of darkness. Although he had previously scorned photography, Brassaï soon realized that the camera was the ideal means with which to capture the fantastic scenes he observed on his nocturnal rambles and, encouraged by ANDRE KERTESZ, he began to photograph the underworld in about 1930.

Sometimes with a friend, but usually alone, Brassaï photographed prostitutes, transvestites of both sexes, lovers, sewer cleaners, and street toughs. He went backstage at the Folies-Bergère, attended the annual *Bal des Quat'z Artes*, and even accompanied cesspool cleaners on their midnight rounds. Brassaï believed that the customs and activities he observed were rooted in traditions reaching far back into the city's past and he was fearless in his pursuit of the elusive characters who peopled this secret society. Access to their world was very often difficult and dangerous. He was threatened, had his wallet stolen, and on one occasion, after a particularly successful night of picture-taking at a dance hall, his bag filled with exposed negatives disappeared.

Using a 6.5 × 9cm Voigtlander camera on a tripod, Brassaï made his nocturnal photographs with a flashbulb if the available light was too dim. Today night photography is nothing special, but in the 1930s it was considered impossible. By these simple means Brassaï made a collection of images which recreate, with unsurpassed intimacy, a world beyond the tourist's grasp. A collection of these, *Paris de Nuit (Paris by Night)* was published in France in 1933.

Brassaï's approach to photographing people was never devious or concealed. He regarded the taking of a photograph as an artistic event and wanted his subjects to be fully aware of the act. He encouraged complicity and disagreed with those who sought to catch their subjects off-guard. In a radio interview, discussing his technique, Brassaï said, 'When I do a picture of someone, I like to render the immobility of the face, of the person thrown back on his inner solitude. The mobility of the face is always an accident. . . . But I hunt for what is permanent.'

Although his photographs function on one level as documents, Brassaï has never seen himself as a photojournalist or documentarian. In an interview in 1976 he explained that a reportage photograph was usually shown with an explanatory caption and unable to stand alone. For Brassaï, 'The structure or composition of a photograph is just as important as its subject. This is not an aesthetic demand but a practical one. Only images powerfully grasped — streamlined — have the capacity to penetrate the memory, to remain there, to become, in a word, unforgettable. It is the sole criterion for a photograph.' Brassaï's images are carefully composed and fully utilize the expressive possibilities of light and shadow.

Like many of his colleagues, in order to

Two Hoodlums *(1932)* Brassaï took most of his photographs by night. These two young toughs, dressed in cloth caps and with defiant looks on their faces, he found in a Paris backstreet. One of Brassaï's best known images, it is a menacing and exciting composition.

support himself, Brassaï occasionally took on commercial assignments. In 1938 he began to work for the American magazine *Harper's Bazaar* where he was originally asked to photograph fashion but refused. Instead, he made portraits of prominent cultural figures, and made a series of pictures of artists in their studios.

Brassaï's talents and interests are varied. He spent 25 years collecting photographs of wall graffitti, and in 1960 published *Graffitti*, a book of 105 black and white photographs. His friendship with Picasso, which dated back to the 1930s, led him to produce two books, *Les Sculptures de Picasso (Picasso's Sculptures)* (1948) and *Picasso and Company* (1966). He has continued to sculpt and paint, and Picasso once likened his drawings to a 'gold mine'.

Although he has excelled at everything he has turned his hand to, it is Brassaï's belief that photography has been his best and most original means of expression. His photographs of an older, different Paris — many of which remain unpublished and unknown to the public — are unique in the history of the medium. The personalities and events of Brassaï's Paris live on.

bill brandt

British/born 1904

"Composition is important but I believe it is largely a matter of instinct...I feel the simplest approach can often be the most effective."

Brandt stands out as arguably one of the greatest forces in twentieth-century photography. His work is multifarious, covering all aspects of image-making; yet throughout, his photographs maintain a strong individuality in both technique and composition.

Born in London in 1904, Bill Brandt lived part of his youth in Germany and Switzerland, and it was not until his early twenties that he became interested in photography. Strongly attracted to the school of modern French photography which had just been accepted by the Surrealist movement, Brandt went to live in Paris where for a short period around 1929 he became a student at MAN RAY'S

146 **Northumbrian miner at his evening meal** *(1930s)* During the 1930s Brandt chronicled all aspects of the English class system and these photographs were published in 1936 in his first book *The English at Home*. Although not reproduced in the book, this image is typical of his early portraits. Brandt was not against his sitters being aware of his presence or even for them to adopt a formal pose. He was concerned however that the subjects and their surroundings should harmonize.

Top Withens, West Riding, Yorkshire *(1945)* This is the landscape which inspired Emily Brontë to write *Wuthering Heights*. Brandt studied the elements carefully before he took a single shot. He was to say later 'When I have seen — or sensed — the atmosphere of my subject, I try to convey that atmosphere by intensifying the elements that compose it.'

studio. The photographers he particularly admired at this time were ATGET, Man Ray, BRASSAI and, later, CARTIER-BRESSON and EDWARD WESTON.

In 1931 Brandt returned to London, and, until the beginning of the Second World War, set about chronicling the various social stratas that made up the English class system. In his first book *The English at Home*, 1936, a complete resumé is given of the English people and, their environments, from the Depression-torn existence of the working classes in London's East End and northern mining communities, to the lavish excesses of England's aristocracy.

Throughout these images there remains an integrity for the subject far beyond mere reportage. Adding to the dramatic content, strong deep blacks begin to appear in Brandt's photographs, brought about by full printing on high contrast papers. On printing Brandt was later to write in *Camera in London*: 'Intensification of my effects is often done in the process of printing. Each subject must determine its own treatment. I consider it essential that the photographer should do his own printing

148

Francis Bacon walking on Primrose Hill, London *(1963)* Fully printed on high contrast papers, as with many of his images, the dramatic effect of Brandt's portraits of mid-twentieth-century writers, artists and poets is heightened by the fact that he rarely shows his subject smiling.

Nude *(1953)* With a whole-plate mahogany Kodak Angle camera, Brandt started to photograph nudes in the mid-1940s, a project that has fascinated him to the present. By unorthodox positioning of the camera and the use of ultra wide-angle lenses, Brandt has deliberately distorted the body's form.

and enlarging. The final effect of the finished print depends so much on these operations.'

During these pre-war years Brandt contributed to various international publications including *Illustrated, Picture Post, Verve* and the Surrealist magazine *Minotaure*. In 1938 his first one-man show was organized by the Arts et Métiers Graphiques, resulting in his second book *A Night in London*, published the same year.

Between 1940 and 1941 Brandt was commissioned by the Home Office Records Department to record the effects of the blackouts on London and its inhabitants. By moonlight he photographed the city skyline with the dark silhouettes of buildings precisely delineated by exposures of 20 or even up to 30 minutes; the large terraced buildings and people in the Underground air raid shelters and basements. The photographs were published by the magazine *Lilliput* in 1942.

The 1940s also heralded many of Brandt's finest landscapes. *Top Withens, West Riding, Yorkshire*, the setting for Emily Brontë's *Wuthering Heights*, taken in the depths of a 1945 winter, is no accident of composition. The wild, threatening sky and frosted gale-blown grasses encapsulate perfectly the tensions of Brontë's novel and underline Brandt's careful sense of timing. Brandt would explore and contemplate the correct setting for his landscapes before attempting a single shot, returning to a venue months or years later to achieve the correct elemental conditions. Brandt feels that, for him, composition is largely a matter of instinct, and to follow the 'rules' is to limit the imagination. On seeing his subject, Brandt has a definite, preconceived idea of the effect he wishes to achieve. This, in turn, determines his approach, as he states in *Camera in London*: 'To give the impression of the immensity of a building, I approach close to some small architectural detail, photographing it from such an angle that the lines of the building run into the far distance, giving a feeling of infinity. I may want to convey an impression of loneliness of a human figure in an outdoor scene. Taking that figure close to the camera and on a path stretching away behind him to a distant horizon intensifies the effect of solitude.' Brandt feels that the simplest approach is usually the most effective and that a subject is most forcibly presented when set squarely in the picture frame, without fussy or distracting surroundings.

Throughout his career, Brandt has compiled a large selection of portraits of contemporary poets, writers and artists. He always tries to locate his subjects in surroundings synonymous with their work, achievements or life-style, and some of his

earliest portraits done in the 1940s and 1950s — Dylan Thomas, Robert Graves, E M Forster, Edith and Osbert Sitwell, Graham Greene and Henry Moore — clearly illustrate this point. Printed with high tonal contrast, the dramatic effect in these portraits is emphasized by the fact that Brandt would rarely photograph his subjects smiling or laughing, preferring them to concentrate on the more serious aspects of life. There is no set format for positioning the sitters in his portraits, for example those of Georges Braque, Jean Dubuffet or Francis Bacon present the sitter towards the extremities of the picture, emphasizing background detail and giving depth and perspective to the images. Using a Rolleiflex or Hasselblad, Brandt would shoot 12 shots in rapid succession, not allowing his subject to adopt a stock pose, illustrating his feelings that 'composition should never become an obsession'.

Marjorie Beckett writes of Brandt's portraits in Brandt's book *Shadow of Light* that Brandt makes extensive use of rooms and backgrounds, working quickly and with intense concentration. He seeks to capture more than a fleeting impression of a snapshot and 'thinks a good portrait should have a profound likeness.'

Inspired by Orson Welles' film *Citizen Kane* and its unusual use of interior sets, Brandt's fascination with rooms became a major force as a backdrop to many of his nude series of pictures. He acquired an old Kodak whole-plate angle camera and began photographing nudes in the mid-1940s. The camera, fitted with an extreme wide-angle lens, had what would seem to be a fairly limited usefulness in that it would exaggerate perspective by increasing the size of foreground objects disproportionately to those in the distance. And yet the photographer must have jumped for joy on the realization of these effects, after the first experiments with this camera. By masterful positioning of the camera, the model in these early pictures is wildly distorted into the confines of the environment. Using a less cumbersome Hasselblad, Brandt moved his model to a beach, blending the body's form to become an integral part of the landscape. In 1961 his book *Perspective of Nudes* was published, but this in no way marked the end of the project with *Brandt Nudes 1945–80* being his latest offering.

It is conjecture to label these images as extensions of Brandt's earlier associations with the Surrealist movement as the equipment used contributed, to no small extent, to the remarkably distorted effects. It is Brandt's overriding empathy with his surroundings and subjects, whether it be reportage, landscapes, portraits or nudes, that is the key factor behind his success.

149

ansel adams

American/born 1902

"My approach to photography is based on my belief in the aspects of grandeur and of the minutiae all about us."

Ansel Adams.is the author of America's most stately landscape photographs. The best known of these may be *Moonrise, Hernandez, New Mexico 1944*, an image of a straggling village, church and cemetery on a dark plain backed by a distant mountain range, and all aligned in narrow bands under a vast sky. His images are mainly of the American West, of mountainous and unpeopled landscapes in California, Wyoming, New Mexico and Arizona. Sometimes his work has taken him further afield, to Alaska and Hawaii in 1947 and 1948 to photograph National Parks, but his main subject has been Western landscape.

150   **Dawn, Great Smoky Mountains National Park** *(1948)* Photography, notoriously, takes things in passing, as they happen. It appears ideally suited to catch the dawn or any other particular time of day. But in this photograph Ansel Adams symbolizes the dawn, in an image of a pervasive darkness touched by points of light. Pictures such as this, which slowly modulate between light and darkness, give an impression of a cohesion, in which disruptive contrasts have been resolved.

Boards and Thistles *(1932)* At the beginning of the twentieth century photographers made pictures of distinguished subjects which declared natural harmonies clearly. But in the 1920s, inspired by the new idea of 'photographic seeing', derived from the teaching of Alfred Stieglitz, they began to scrutinize commonplace material, arguing that it too, if rightly looked at, was beautiful. Writing retrospectively in 1940, Adams stated that 'Stieglitz would never say that certain objects of the world were more or less beautiful than others — telegraph poles, for instance, compared with oak trees. He would accept them for what they are . . .

Other, and very distinguished, American photographers have worked with these same landscapes, most notably Adams' friend EDWARD WESTON, with whom he photographed in the High Sierra in 1937. Yet Adams' pictures have characteristics all their own. He searches for, and achieves, largeness; he finds forms which do justice to immensity. His horizons are distant, extended and topped by large skies. Often he underlines immensity by the inclusion of small but significant details on nearer ground: a horse, for instance, grazing by trees in a patch of sunlight under a range of jagged mountains, or the delicate buildings of Hernandez in their huge setting.

Adams works with an especial regard for balance. His America may be large and largely unspoiled, but it can hardly be described as wild. He finds and shows terrain in which the severities of rock and snow are mitigated by the mildness of still water and vegetation. His skies only rarely open onto the infinite; mists and drifting clouds intervene and bring with them intimations of caprice and imagination. He envisages America as something very close to paradise, rich in rivers, woods and wind-blown grass, and decorated by such natural beauties as that of the dawn light touching springtime woods.

152

Adams' photographs are in sharp focus, brilliantly realized. The images tend to depict microscopic details of stone, wood-grain, bark, ice, lichen and drifted sand. He calls this 'a clean, straightforward approach to photography', but argues that it involves far more than technical exactitude. What it really does involve he is reluctant to say, and for very good reasons. If words could serve adequately then they would be used, but words are unreliable, and likely to obscure more than they reveal. Some recent aesthetic theories, in particular those connected with romanticism, admit to a suspicion of words and hope instead for direct access to all important nature. Photography, with its ability to take transcriptions from nature, allows just such direct access; but, in the late 1920s, some artists felt that it had been misused, and that 'pictorial' photography, made in imitation of painting and etching, was a betrayal of the medium's truth-telling capacities.

The last time Adams associated his work with the term 'pictorial' was in January 1931 when he exhibited 'Pictorial Photographs of the Sierra Nevada Mountains' at the Smithsonian Institution, Washington DC. By 1931 he was dissatisfied with his pictures from the 1920s, even though they had been acclaimed. He recalls various turning points around that time, one of which was a meeting with

**Mount McKinley
and Wonder Lake**
(1947) In 1947
Adams photo-
graphed in National
Parks in Hawaii and
Alaska, where he
pictured the land-
scape as big,
beautiful and orderly.
He mitigated bulk
by distance, rock by
water, and generally
established spatial
continuities across
rippling prairie
grass, the surfaces
of lakes and the
flanks of mountains.
Yet at the same time
as he celebrated the
original landscape
he made complicated
pictures, like this in
which he plays with
a normal order of
things, showing a
white mountain in a
dark sky, and
matching snow in an
even whiter lake.

153

PAUL STRAND at Taos, New Mexico, in 1930. Strand was already an established artist, whose pictures had been published in 1917 by ALFRED STIEGLITZ in his magazine *Camera Work*. Nancy Newhall, Adams' biographer, notes that he was impressed by the 'intense incandescence' of Strand's negatives, and by the 'cool clarity' of prints by Edward Weston,

In 1931 he decided to begin all over again, and committed himself to 'the simple dignity of the glossy print', putting aside textured photographic papers. He became, in his own words, acutely conscious of 'the continuous beauty of the things that are', and remained so.

In 1932 he helped found the well-known Group f.64, which took its name from the smallest stop available on a large format camera. At f.64 the aperture produced images with great clarity and depth of focus. The group, of 11 photographers including Imogen Cunningham, Edward Weston and his son, Brett, exhibited only

once together, in San Francisco towards the end of 1932, and continued to meet informally until 1935.

His writing in 1932 is that of a romantic who feels deeply in front of the earth's beauties: 'A spirit of unearthly beauty moved in the darkness and spoke in terms of song and the frail music of violins.' His photographs, such as *Boards and Thistles* — made in 1932 and exhibited at the f.64 show in that year — often invite a more dispassionate response. Adams wrote about this in an undated note, cited by Nancy Newhall: 'If I have any credo, it may be this: if I choose to photograph a rock, I must present a rock . . . the print must augment and enlarge the experience of a rock . . . stress tone and texture . . . yet never, under any conditions, "dramatize" the rock, nor suggest emotional or symbolic connotations other than what is obviously associated with the rock.'

Seen in retrospect, Adams' career seems inevitable, as though the beauties of the

American land demanded and found an admirer. Yet in 1930 there was nothing inevitable about either Adams' style or subject matter. American artists at that time turned their attention to the American people and to society, and worked towards national self-awareness and social improvement. Photographic purism of the sort practised by Adams was a minority interest, supported in California and by the aged Alfred Stieglitz in New York. That the purist tradition in landscape survived and gathered strength into the 1950s is, in some measure, Ansel Adams' doing. After Stieglitz he is probably the most influential of all American photographers, as lecturer, technician and artist. Harry Callahan, a major artist in photography over recent decades, admits apropos his formative years: 'Ansel is what freed me.' He freed others too, and more importantly moved landscape to the centre of American photography, where it has remained more or less up to the present.

154

Statue and Oil Derricks, Signal Hill, Long Beach, California *(1939)*
The bulk of Adams' work has been in praise of natural landscape in the American West. Like Paul Strand and Edward Weston, he had reservations about the encroachments of industrial culture. In this image a mourning figure with a garland sits in isolation in a landscape which industry has begun to dominate. Such a stark opposition between light and darkness, ideal and ungainly, is unusual in Adams' work.

Rails and Jet Trails, Roseville, California *(1953)*
Adams' pictures are often of harmonious, balanced landscapes — of rock and water, dead and living tissue. Here marks in the sky are rhymed with inscriptions on the land, and a signalling disc stands in the sky as a black sun. As in a piece of music, themes are stated and reiterated in different modes, organic and swirling marks are set against the rectilinear systems of an industrial landscape. It is an example of a sophisticated composition drawn out of everyday material.

richard avedon

American/born 1923

**" The photographs have a reality for me that
people don't. It's through the photographs
that I know them. "**

Richard Avedon's photography has but
one subject – the men and women whose
images come into focus through his lens.
Their looks, gestures, vanities and weak-
nesses are the exclusive object of his
attentions. However, Avedon has so far
shown no interest in the general public.
On the contrary, he seems bewitched by a
limited spectrum of humanity. On the one
hand, there are the stunning models –
each one an embodiment of her era –
whom he has transformed into the per-
sonification of glamour and beauty through
40 years of fashion photography; on the
other are the celebrities and figures of

156 **The Duke and
Duchess of
Windsor** *(1957)*
Flattery was not
Avedon's goal in
this portrait of the
Windsors. The
couple are seen in
all their human frailty
in this characteristic
example of Avedon's
supposedly frank,
yet somehow savage
style of portraiture.

Dovima *(1955)*
Avedon chose to
photograph the
model Dovima, in a
dress by Christian
Dior, in the Cirque
d'Hiver, Paris,
before the massive,
incongruous bodies
of the circus
elephants. The result
is an extraordinary
image which well
exemplifies the
extravagant,
inspired scenarios
created by Avedon
in the 1950s, before
he abandoned
location work in
favour of the
artificially-lit plain
back-drops of his
New York studio.

power, the subjects of Avedon's harsh and supposedly frank portraits. The bright-eyed young man who rose to fame as a fashion photographer in the 1940s and 1950s with a dazzling *repertoire* of ideas; the mercurial, spirited young photographer who injected new zest into fashion photography, Avedon has matured into a portraitist who pursues his subjects in a harsh style with missionary zeal.

The paradoxes within Avedon's work are countless and unfathomable, and the photographer is reluctant to unlock the secrets of his intentions. While many truths may lie beneath the superficialities of Avedon's fashion and beauty work, critics have commented that the 'realism' of his portraits is, after all, only another form of artifice. To this Avedon throws back a quote from Diane Arbus, that a photograph is '. . . a secret about a secret.' He discloses nothing and leaves people to gauge their own experiences and reactions. Both fashion and portraiture have vied for his attention, and, although Avedon may bestow greater value upon his portraits, it is as a brilliant, consistently inventive and highly attuned chronicler of the changing tastes of fashion and beauty that Avedon deserves to be acclaimed.

Richard Avedon was born in New York in 1923 and learned photography in the US Navy. His introduction to fashion photography was effected by the brilliant art director of *Harper's Bazaar*, Alexey Brodovitch, who spotted Avedon's nascent talent under his tutelage at New York's New School for Social Research. Avedon's work first appeared in the pages of *Harper's* in 1945, and he was to remain under contract to the magazine for 20 years. In 1966 he changed allegiance and entered into a contract with *Vogue*, for whom he is still a prolific and exciting contributor.

Avedon's debut coincided with the re-birth of Paris after the war years as a fashion and cultural centre and amongst the most sparkling of his early fashion essays were photographs of the Paris collections done on location. Avedon's hero had been Martin Munkacsi, the first photographer to inject life and movement into a formerly static and formalized genre and, like Munkasci, Avedon made his models live – they laughed, flirted, jumped puddles, climbed from taxis, and visited night-clubs. They were glamorous and classy, and very far removed from the lifeless pre-war models.

Avedon's technique was always faultless, and effects of limited focal depth or the haziness of movement were always deliberate choices; the spontaneity was carefully orchestrated. Many of the photographs from this first phase are like stills from a filmed sequence with each image

giving a clue, as it were, to a more complex scenario. As Avedon's fashion work evolved, not only did it become more simplified, but it became restricted by the arbitrary limitations of the studio. Avedon abandoned location work and daylight, feeling that the strobe light was more 'honest' in a modern context. CECIL BEATON wrote in *The Magic Image* (1975) that Avedon said of his former love for daylight 'It's like loving something from long ago that I can't believe in any more. It would be a lie for me to photograph the daylight in a world of Hiltons, airports, supermarkets and television. Daylight is something I rarely see – something I must give up – like childhood.' His models were still full of energy, leaping and striding across his backdrops, but they, like the subjects of his straight portraiture, who were made to stand and never allowed to sit or relax before his camera, were now confined within a totally abstracted and harshly-lit environment. This was not so much the modern world of airports and supermarkets as the tormented, enclosed world of Avedon's view of humanity.

The 1970s saw the emergence of a new idea of beauty in Avedon's fashion work. The healthy, seemingly natural looks of models such as Lauren Hutton, Janice Dickinson and Patti Hansen are captured in uncluttered compositions which belie the minute care and preparation which Avedon puts into the creation of each image. During the 1970s, Avedon also attracted considerable attention for his portrait work, with a major exhibition at the Marlborough Gallery, New York, in 1975, and the publication of the book *Portraits* in 1976. The portraits have tremendous impact, an effect heightened by his tight cropping and, in certain cases, by the use of giant, life-size, mural-like prints. Avedon the portraitist is an unflinching observer, and his method helps create the disarming rapport which leads to the image as a moment of truth. For his portraits Avedon uses a 10 × 8in Deardorff camera: having focused, he stands by the camera, facing his subject in a direct, eye-to-eye confrontation thus forcing, he maintained in a magazine interview in 1977, '. . . a *real* connection between me and the person I am photographing. . . . It is a collaboration,' he conceded, 'that involves trust and sometimes betrayal.' He also admitted that the portraits are '. . . more a definition of myself than of someone else – a portrait of what I know, what I feel, what I'm afraid of.'

Avedon's energy as a photographer is similar to the twin poles of a magnet, each existing only by virtue of its constant, perfect opposition to the other, interdependent yet irreconcilable.

Patti Hansen *(1977)* Here, one of the top American models of the late 1970s is modelling fashions by Versace. The photograph was published in American *Vogue* in July 1977. Simplicity has become the hallmark of Avedon's fashion work, but it is a deceptive simplicity. Patti Hansen's healthy, glowing good looks contrast with the haughty, stylized features of Dovima, but Ms Hansen's 'look' is just as meticulously put together by the photographer.

robert frank

Swiss/born 1924

"To me photography is life. It has to deal with life."

The publication of Robert Frank's book *The Americans* in 1958 revolutionized and revitalized photography. Apart from providing a critical insight into aspects of American life which did not conform to the 'American Dream' — the casual, unglamorous moments of everyday life, the desolation and melancholy inherent in big cities — Frank created a new way of seeing through dramatic, dynamic, blurred or tilted shots. As an outsider, Frank's was an authentic view of a society down-at-heel surrounded by the superficial trappings of materialism.

Robert Frank was born in Switzerland in 1924, and after working as a photographer in Paris, emigrated to America in 1946. He began working for magazines such as *Harper's Bazaar* under the guidance of Alexey Brodovitch, before turning to reportage. However, the rigid requirements of the magazines and agencies were not to Frank's liking and after a trip to Europe with EDWARD STEICHEN in 1953 to collect photographs for the 'Post-war European Photographers' exhibition, he applied for a Guggenheim Fellowship. With the help of WALKER EVANS he became the first European to be given the award, and with it the financial freedom to travel round the United States.

In 1955, Vladimir Nabokov's highly controversial novel *Lolita* was published in France. The United States was equally scandalized by the photographs from Frank's journey, which are a searing indictment of American society. Yet, despite their bitterness, they are not pessimistic in attitude. In the introduction to the American edition, published in 1959, the American beat novelist, Jack Kerouac, wrote of 'The humor, the sadness, the EVERYTHING-ness and American-ness of these pictures!' and in the same year Frank himself wrote, 'Black and white is the vision of hope and despair'. Both extremes are included in his photographs. As early as 1951, the theme of the tension between life and death appears, and is one which recurs in much of Frank's work. People at funerals, car accidents, or standing around doing nothing, in melancholy bars or nightmare streets — the despondency of these photographs is distilled into

London *(1951)*
A child runs down the street away from the hearse with its wide open door. The composition is simple yet there is an apparent tension between the two; the spontaneity of life and the inevitability of death. Such stark, symbolic contrasts recur in Frank's work, but never overwhelm the realism and immediacy of the images. The grainy surface of the print adds to the realistic atmosphere of an empty street on a wet and gloomy day, while the sharp diagonals, leading to a vanishing point to the very left, accentuate the dramatic impact.

LONDON 1951

162

Beaufort, South Carolina *(1958)*
A jukebox looms over the child on the floor. A calm domestic interior, composed in the classic manner of Walker Evans, has been disturbed by this incongruous object, its ornate decoration jarring with the unadorned and simple furniture of the wooden shack. The child is oblivious of all this. The sunlight coming through the window is pleasant, and the freshness of the place counteracts the imaginary threat of the sinister machine.

a vision which, ultimately, is not negative, but depicts with great sensitivity and affection the courage of people and their ability to endure. This is a very different kind of optimism from that seen in Steichen's exhibition, 'The Family of Man', 1955, in which humanity was depicted as an integrated family. Frank showed the disintegration of society, the isolation of man, but also his dignity and nobility in the face of despair. The photographs are an affirmation of life, and Frank's criticism of society arises out of love, not hate or disillusionment.

Frank's technique perfectly complements his unique vision. The major influences on his work are Walker Evans, with his understanding of the significance of mundane objects and classical sense of composition, and BILL BRANDT, with his surreal, poetic, and documentary style. Writing about form in his book *Denver*, the American topographic photographer Robert Adams spoke of 'a tension so exact that it is peace.' To this electric calm Frank adds deliberate imperfections with grainy, out-of-focus, angled shots which contravene all the canons of composition and printing; it is these very 'flaws' which animate the photographs making them more alive and more violent. Frank wrote of his attempt 'To show what I felt seeing those faces, those people, the kind of hidden violence'. As well as revealing the tensions underlying society in the United States during the McCarthy era, Frank's photo-

graphs deliberately violate expectations and undermine complacency, forcing the observer to see things as they really are, not as portrayed in glossy magazines.

The same objects recur again and again in Frank's photographs: jukeboxes, coffins, bars, lifts, dustbins, televisions and automobiles; he is fascinated by the paraphernalia of a consumer society, but even more fascinated by the way in which people become attached to these objects. The anxiety seen in so many of Frank's faces stems from the alienation of city life, and the isolation of the individual in the crowd is that much more acute. The loneliness of the figure is accentuated by swiftly moving, blurred forms but the pathos is matched by a humour, affection and poetry which is summed up in the conclusion to Kerouac's introduction: 'Robert

Bar, New York City *(1958)* The main source of light in this image is the jukebox which seems to have a glowing life of its own. Two people sit in an obscure corner while a third man exits hastily. The violent, blurred movement of his arm intensifies the atmosphere to give the true feel of the place.

163

Frank, Swiss, unobtrusive, nice, with that little camera that he raises and snaps with one hand, he sucked a sad poem right out of America onto film, taking rank among the tragic poets of the world.'

Given the cinematic nature of Frank's photographs with their drama and sense of movement, it was a logical, if not fortuitous step for him to abandon still photography when he lost his Leica and turn to film-making. Kerouac and the beat poet Allen Ginsberg collaborated on Frank's first film *Pull My Daisy* (1959–60) 'a spontaneous documentary of life among the beatniks'. Like his photographs, this film with its absence of plot, non-actors, improvisation and general craziness broke all the rules of film-making. The film is as zany and humorous as any of Ginsberg's poems, and as iconoclastic as the abstract ex-

pressionist paintings of Frank's artist friends de Kooning and Kline. Frank was at the centre of avant-garde and underground life in New York City, and his uncompromising photographic statements spoke directly to the rebellious generation of the 1960s. Since then he has continued to make films, and now lives in Nova Scotia, Canada.

There is an appealing urgency and emotional commitment in Frank's photographs and films. As well as being authentic documents of the turbulent times in which he lived, his work makes a very personal and positive statement. The integrity of his ironic approach produces the kind of tragic vision which reconciles hope and despair; he has succeeded in his efforts 'to transform destiny into awareness.'

norman parkinson

British/born 1913

"I like to make people look as good as they'd like to look, and with luck a shade better."

Born in 1913 Norman Parkinson's photo graphic career began in 1931 when he left Westminster School, London, to become apprenticed to the 'court photographer', Speaight of Bond Street. For the payment of a £300 premium, he learned the fundamental skills of photography, assisted in the darkroom, and focused the cumbersome studio camera, all for £1 per week. Parkinson served only two of his three year apprenticeship, because he felt restricted by the rigid techniques and unimaginative methods of the studio.

At the age of 21, backed by his great aunts, he opened his own studio at 1, Dover Street just off Piccadilly, London. Here he mounted his camera on wheels and devised a flexible arrangement of lights based on the system used in film studios; the moveable spots and flood-lights could be angled to produce shadows and effects which made major and time-

164

Fashion photograph for the cover of British *Vogue* (March 1949) The arrangement of the two figures both looking out of the picture frame in opposite directions produces an effective dynamic tension to the composition. The man in the background is deliberately out of focus to give the scene depth and suggest an imagined storyline and relationship between the two figures. The handling of the colour and the use of a limited range of brown and whites shows Parkinson's confident restraint and provides the ideal background to Wenda Rogerson's bright red lipstick which becomes one of the focal points. The photograph was taken in the *Vogue* studios using natural light.

Fashion photograph for British *Vogue* (April 1950) The model is Norman Parkinson's wife Wenda Rogerson. She is dressed in Molyneux's caramel satin evening dress against a 1907 Silver Ghost in the Rolls Royce show-rooms. The use of a silver Rolls to show off the luxury of the satin dress is a good example of Parkinson's restrained yet sumptuous use of colour where the subject requires it. The inclusion of a red rose in the model's hand is the only concession to an otherwise rich monochromatic colour scheme. The photograph was taken with a Linhof studio camera on ½ plate Ektachrome daylight film.

consuming re-touching of the finished portrait unnecessary.

Most of Parkinson's sitters were young debutantes, and although he experimented with specially constructed settings and backgrounds, after a short while the work became limiting and unsatisfying. Fortunately, in 1935 he was commissioned by the British edition of *Harper's Bazaar* to photograph a series of hat fashions out of doors. Parkinson bought a 5 × 4in Graflex for £17 and, finding freedom away from the confines of the studio, produced an entirely new concept of fashion photography which has since been called 'action realism'. This approach was pioneered by Martin Munkasci and Jean Moral, but as Parkinson was unaware of their work, he created his own instinctive style.

Parkinson's first photographs showed girls walking in pairs in Hyde Park, strolling past Buckingham Palace or striding purposefully up and down the streets of Edinburgh. His aim was to take moving pictures with a still camera and this approach showed fashion in a newly accessible and credible light. Parkinson's work contrasted sharply with the indoor, flower-strewn concoctions of elegant artifice which had previously been the norm of studio work. 'My women behaved differently . . .', he recalls, 'my women went shopping, drove cars, had children, kicked the dog . . .

Parkinson continued working for *Harper's* until the outbreak of the war, but also had a large volume of work published in the *Bystander* including lively reportage essays on subjects like Wimbledon tennis tournaments, car race track meetings and a series on Welsh miners and their families during the Depression. Other assignments included a pictorial record of the 1939 New York World's Fair and the 1937 Paris *Exposition Universelle*.

Parkinson spent the war years working on his farm in Gloucestershire, which he combined with reconnaissance photography over France with the Royal Air Force. After the war, Parkinson began work for Condé Nast, specifically for the British and American editions of *Vogue*, to which he has continued to contribute throughout the years. His work has also appeared in a wide variety of international periodicals such as *Life*, *Look* and *Town and Country*.

In the 1940s, Parkinson's fashion photographs of models in natural settings such as railway stations, against London landmarks or in the Royal Crescent at Bath had a far-reaching influence on other photographers. His New York colour photograph *Park Avenue* showing a model in profile against the speeding blur of a yellow taxi set a trend in the United States for out of door fashion photography. Over

the years, the various locations used in Parkinson's fashion photographs have grown steadily more exotic, always keeping one step ahead of tourist hordes, with memorable locations including anywhere from the steppes of Russia to the arid deserts of Monument Valley in Utah.

Gradually, Parkinson's style has become familiar through his use of a number of recurring trademarks. One favourite approach is to shoot *contre-jour* (against the light) using a fill-in foreground flash. 'Most of the pictures I take into the sun, then I can control the light. Work the other way round and you're lost.' Another trait found in his earliest pictures which he still uses from time to time, is the placement of a blurred foreground figure at the edge of the composition which adds depth and increases the viewer's involvement in the scene. Parkinson's pictures always have spontaneity, lightness of touch, and frequently an amusing scene taking place in the background: the elegant model's dogs are rather too friendly, a pile of hat boxes are precariously balanced in a footman's arms as he tries to keep up with his ladyship, or, in a famous 1960 photograph, three laughing, black-grimed miners hold aloft a startled model in her best new dress.

Parkinson is now known primarily as a colour photographer. His first colour work, taken on 35mm Kodachrome film, appeared in *Harper's Bazaar* in the 1930s. Although he occasionally produces dazzlingly complex colour schemes, in his best work the colour is restricted to a limited tonal range. These pictures are impressive in their purity and restraint, as when, for example, in a 1980 edition of the French *Vogue*, a model in a pure white draped dress is posed beside a cream marble sculpture from Olympia against a background of cool grey.

Before each shot Parkinson will shoot several packs of Polaroid film in order to adjust the exposure and frame the subject; 'I haven't used an exposure meter for 20 years,' he commented recently. On all assignments he carries two sets of large and small format cameras to cover all eventualities. For carefully composed shots Parkinson will use a tripod-mounted Hasselblad, preferring the $2\frac{1}{4}$in transparency when time allows, but using a motor-driven Nikon when greater speed or spontaneity is required for the 'snatch' shot.

As early as 1935, in a series of photographs of the liner 'The Queen Mary', Parkinson experimented with the effects produced by double exposures, and since then has from time to time returned to this with varying degrees of success. One of the best series of double exposures were taken to show the 1961 'Dior look' for

Queen magazine, of which Parkinson was an associate editor from 1960 to 1964. For the Dior pictures he first exposed the film of the night lights of the Place de La Concorde, and then photographed the dresses in the studio on the same film.

Known mainly as a fashion photographer, Parkinson nevertheless has achieved a certain reputation as a portraitist, a field to which he devotes about one tenth of his working hours. 'I try to make people as good as they'd like to look, and with luck a shade better. . . . If I photograph a woman then my job is to make her as beautiful as it is possible for her to be. If I photograph a gnarled old man, then I must make him as interesting as a gnarled old man can be.' While these two statements may sum up Parkinson's attitude, they belie the wide variety of portrait studies he has made. The massive presence of John Huston playing cards on the set of the film of *Moby Dick*, the simple but powerfully realized head of Lord David Cecil placed against a plain background, Beatrice Lillie surprised and animated at the Café de Paris, the close-up head and alert eyes of Walter de la Mare, and the timeless elegance of Ava Gardner in her 1950s off-the-shoulder gown are all examples of Parkinson's ability to catch, in a split second, the essence of the sitter in a convincingly natural and spontaneous way.

Always dismissive of the claims of photography as an art, Parkinson views it simply as a craft, and refers to his own work only as snapshots. Describing his formula for success in the 1962 annual *New Photograms*, Parkinson sums up his attitude to photography in a lighthearted manner, which typically belies his serious approach: 'Photography is not an art! . . . a photographer is an engine-driver — get there on time! A poet maybe, a do-it-yourself chemist — mostly in the dark, a a diplomatist with the client who has been given a wonderful picture and can't see it, a journalist who uses his nut, and quickly. If a photographer is all of these things, then he is moving on — success is with him, or just around the corner.'

John Huston
(1955) Taken on assignment for *Vogue* magazine on the set of the film *Moby Dick*, which was being made in Britain at that time, this portrait was captured with a Rolleiflex and lit by a 2000 watt bulb which illuminated the scene from the top left corner.

Parkinson took the photograph by positioning his camera at ground level to convey the massive looming presence of John Huston, who almost totally fills the composition, a study in intense concentration as he plays cards for high stakes with the film's stunt men.

helmut newton
German-born Australian/born 1920

"Newton will not accept anything less than absolute professionalism."

Over the last decade, Helmut Newton has earned a reputation – and attracted a certain notoriety – for his brilliance in an area of photography which he might well be said to have invented. Newton is a fashion photographer, a creator of images of female beauty and eroticism, an astute and amused observer of the mores, the habitat, proclivities and poses of a privileged sector of Western society. His uniqueness stems from his being all of these things at once, with the result that his 'straight' fashion photographs often have an edge of eroticism or cynical wit, and his nudes the poise and stylishness of top fashion models. His erotic portraits are of celebrities of the *beau monde*, and his scenarios, however seemingly bizarre or fantastic, in fact derive their impact from reality, in things observed and judiciously recorded in notebooks for future reference.

Newton has only scorn for the 'fine art'

168   **Model in gym**
(1974) This highly erotic image was taken in a gymnasium in Paris' exclusive Avenue Foch. It was one of a series on the theme of women excercising and undergoing beauty treatments, published in the summer 1974 issue of *Vogue Hommes*. It is a clever image, photographed through the plane of a reflecting mirror-glass wall. Its strength, however, is in the over-powering erotic tension which emanates from the naked figure, stretched provocatively on the weight-lifting frame.

Paloma Picasso
(1973) This young woman, daughter of Pablo Picasso, is presented by Newton as full of character, a creature at once tough and sensual. Her baring of one breast in her black Karl Lagerfeld dress expresses and symbolizes her Amazonian qualities. Her barbaric, heavy gold jewellery, her own design, further emphasizes the particular aspects of his subject which Newton has chosen to depict in what is surely one of his most powerful and successful portraits.

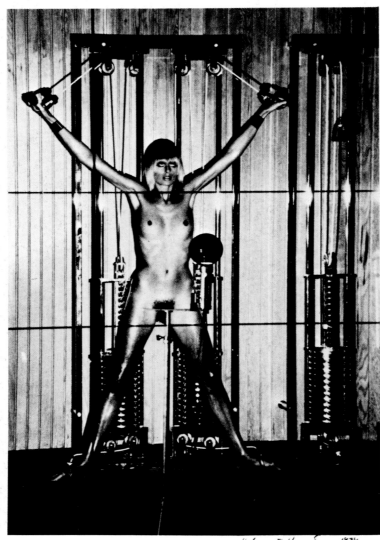

school of photography and for what he sees as its misguided devotion to form rather than content. For Newton, subject matter is all, and formal concerns are pursued only to give full value to the content of his images. He dismisses discussions of good and bad taste by refusing to admit the existence of a distinct division between the erotic and the pornographic, and readily admits elements of vulgarity which fascinate him and give spice to his work. For Newton, banality would represent a more serious accusation than vulgarity. He dismisses such discussions and the accusations levelled at him by those shocked by his work with the assurance of one whose vision is mature, shrewd and pin-sharp, and whose instinctive visual sophistication is the surest riposte.

Born and brought up in Berlin, the son of prosperous Jewish parents, Helmut Newton has been professionally involved in photography for five decades, since the age of 16 when he abandoned his studies and was apprenticed in the studio of Yva. The apprenticeship was cut short when he was forced to leave Berlin in 1938 after his father's arrest by the Gestapo. He then made his way to Australia, spent the war years in the army and, returning to civilian life, resumed his career as a fashion photographer, although this proved to be an uphill struggle. Newton met and married an Australian, and the couple travelled during the 1950s between London, Australia and Paris in search of a base for his work. Their first stay in Paris was in 1958 and, captivated by the city, they returned in 1961 to make it their permanent home.

Paris has proved to be the perfect environment for Newton. It is a city which combines a fastidious concern with the fashionable, and a great respect for traditions; a city with a bourgeoisie and *demi-monde* which he has found fascinating; a city which has provided an ideal point of departure for regular trips to the brash, modern United States which he adores, and the grand European resorts of the wealthy such as Monte Carlo and the Villa d'Este, the backdrop for so many of his pictures.

Newton was already distinctive as a fashion photographer of the 1960s, but the turning point in his career came in the autumn of 1971 when, after recovering from a near-fatal heart attack, he emerged with a new set of priorities, determined to take more photographs for himself and carry through the themes and undercurrents apparent in his work of the 1960s. There was to be no more frenetic and exhausting coverage of the couture collections and through the 1970s Newton has accepted only work which has amused or excited him, or allowed him to create images of a fashion-conscious, glamorous, often perverse world which so intrigues him. The crystallization of his mature style has attracted considerable attention. He has published three books, held one-man shows in various cities — from Paris in 1974 to the most recent in Los Angeles in 1980 — has inspired countless imitators, and been the subject of heated debate and controversy.

Newton's style is unmistakable. He has admired a number of photographers including PENN, AVEDON, BRASSAI and SANDER, but he has emerged with qualities unique unto himself. His style is supremely sophisticated, diamond hard, and his images are flawless because, as a perfectionist, Newton will not accept anything less than absolute professionalism. He will say, self-deprecatingly, that he is not a great technician, but this is untrue. He is in perfect control of every stage of his image-making from the choice and disposition of lighting, film, camera and lens, to the meticulous preparation of his models. He works with the most skilled hairdressers and make-up artists, is aware of every nuance towards the attainment of his distinctive look, directs every gesture to inject the tension he desires, and watches every subtlety of light and shade.

In dismissing his abilities as a technician, Newton is in effect saying that technique is the silent partner to his real assets: imagination and sharp observation; technique should be noticed and appreciated only as an afterthought. For Newton, the challenge is that of constantly injecting new ideas and vitality into his fund of imagery and maintaining his justly-earned reputation as a photographer with the ability to arouse and fascinate. Newton has created images for the 1970s as powerful and relevant as those of Penn and Avedon were for the 1950s.

170

171

Lisa Taylor and Jerry Hall *(1974)* A fashion shot for American *Vogue,* illustrating the erotic swimsuits designed by Rudi Gernreich, has become the basis for a stylish and memorable image. Newton has returned to a favourite theme of women fighting in this highly stylized shot of models Lisa Taylor and Jerry Hall on the sands of Key Biscayne, Florida.

irving penn
American/born 1917

Irving Penn's photographs have lasting qualities and his approach to the art is a timeless one. Whatever he may choose to photograph, Penn's overriding concern is for the absolutes which are the true subjects of photography, its essence when the superficialities of style and fashion are stripped away. Despite Penn's obvious fascination with the people and things before his lens, his images are also about the qualities of light and the, analysis of form, pattern and tone. In a career which has spanned four decades, Penn has set his own exacting standards, single-mindedly and passionately pursuing the photographic truths which concern him. The impressive body of work which is the fruit of his labours demonstrates the consistency of his vision, the measure of his earnestness, and has earned him wide acclaim as one of the most distinguished photographers of all time.

Irving Penn was born in New Jersey in 1917. Between 1934 and 1938 he studied at the Philadelphia Museum School of Industrial Art, Pennsylvania, and his drawings were published in *Harper's Bazaar*. Between 1940 and 1941 he worked as advertising designer for a New York department store before embarking in 1942 on a painting trip to Mexico. Upon his return a year later, Penn was invited to take his first photographs for *Vogue* magazine. It was the art director Alex Liberman who sensed the potential in Penn and began a collaboration between the photographer and Condé Nast, publishers of *Vogue*, which was to establish the basis for his career as a photographer. Liberman and *Vogue* were sufficiently en‍lightened to allow Penn maximum creative freedom, and this patronage has been amply rewarded by the many sensitive and stylish spreads he has created for the magazine over the years.

Penn's work falls into three broad categories: fashion, portraiture and still-life. His approach, however, is such that the categories at times tend to overlap and, through the photographer's piercing scrutiny, superficially diverse subjects become inextricably related. Through Penn's lens, a Moroccan's traditional robes are observed with the same respect for hierarchical values and intrinsic beauty as a Balenciaga or a Dior. The velvety petal of a dying flower is analyzed as an object of abstract and absolute beauty in the same spirit as a model's lips or fingernails, or the stylized debris of a meal. Penn is as intent on capturing the presence of a New Guinea tribesman as he is on capturing the spirit of a Picasso, a Colette, a fashion model — or

"**Penn makes everything extremely hard for himself. He employs no gadgets, no special props, nothing but the simplest lighting.**"
(Cecil Beaton)
a London window cleaner.

Penn shot to success, and his work and style dominated the 1950s. A major landmark in his career was the publication in 1960 of his first and still most impressive book, *Moments Preserved*, a brilliant résumé in the form of eight essays in photographs and words of his achievements. This was followed after an interval of 14 years by the publication of *Worlds in a Small Room*; the next book *Inventive Paris Clothes, 1909–1939*, published in 1977, was eclipsed by the superlatively conceived and produced *Flowers*, published in 1980.

Penn has shown his work in a number of exhibitions, with one-man shows at both the Museum of Modern Art and the

Two Guedras *(1971)* Penn has travelled the world, often with his portable daylight studio tent, recording the features and the character of a remarkable variety of ethnic groups, from Hell's Angels to tribesmen. All his subjects present themselves with a considerable dignity. Isolated against Penn's neutral back-drops they participate in the making of images which capture their characteristics.

Lisa Fonssagrives modelling a harlequin coat by Jerry Parniss *(1951)* This stunning fashion photograph was published in the American edition of *Vogue*, on 1 April 1951. Penn has captured the very essence of the sublime artifice and sophistication of high fashion. The qualities of this image transcend the merely fashionable to express in a timeless way the very spirit of fashion.

Metropolitan Museum of Art, New York. His perfectionism and concern for print quality — the latter no doubt heightened by the opportunities he has enjoyed for exhibiting his work — have led to Penn's increasing interest in the making of prints and the revival in 1967 of the archaic platinum process. Using old negatives or creating new images, Penn has created prints of outstanding quality through his painstaking exploration of the platinum process.

The making of a fine print, however, is the last stage of Penn's creative process. Forming the very basis of his skills are his feeling for light and his intense concentration. Penn's ideal light is that which falls into a studio from the north: 'It is,' he claims, 'a light of such penetrating clarity that even a simple object lying by chance in such a light takes on an inner glow, almost a voluptuousness.... Electric lights are a convenience, but they are used, I believe at the expense of that . . . *absolute existence* that a subject has standing before a camera in a north-light studio.'

The intense concentration which Penn builds up when working was described by a *Vogue* editor who worked regularly with him: 'Penn's sittings were psychological struggles for everyone involved. He suffered over these pictures as no fashion deserves being suffered over, . . . my own enthusiastic approach succumbing under his tense, anguished, soul-searching attack.' Every session for Penn — whoever or whatever the subject — is an endeavour to express perfect observation of the subject, which is usually isolated against a characteristic and much-copied neutral back-drop.

Penn seems to keep no secrets and has published detailed explanations of the technical means he uses to achieve a desired result. In his notes to *Worlds in a Small Room*, he tells of his devotion to the Rolleiflex, of the film used for the majority of the photographs — Tri-X — and his methods of rating and developing the film. In introductions to exhibition catalogues he gives, in minute detail, explicit accounts of his skills, including the manipulations involved in the making of platinum prints and permanent pigment colour prints. These are skills, however, that would stand for little without the genius with which Penn uses them to transform deceptively simple compositions into images which, in addition to showing an inherent graphic brilliance and powerful symbolic essence, are magical hymns of light and shade, at once lyrical and incisive.

david bailey
British/born 1938

" Seeing-pictures are to me people, places and
things that are in their own space and not
rearranged by the eye."

David Bailey has achieved something relatively rare among photographers. His
name has become a household word
among his fellow countrymen, although,
perhaps, he is better known for his colourful reputation than for his work. His reputation, however, is the very stuff of popular
legend, for Bailey, born in 1938 in London, is the working class boy, the East
Ender who, despite the many odds stacked
against him, broke into a closed and elitist
world to capture all the prizes of material
success.

Bailey willingly concedes that chance
and circumstance played as important a
role as talent in his meteoric rise to success
as both a chronicler and the personifi-
cation of the 'youth culture' that characterized the 1960s. Brash, disarmingly
blunt, deliberately unsophisticated and
iconoclastic, Bailey and his contemporaries
would admit to little respect for tradition.
It was Bailey who played out the role of
the fashion photographer-hero and was
the prototype for the photographer-hero
in *Blow-Up*, Antonioni's 1967 film which
explored the ambiguities between image
and reality. Today, the myth is more than
tarnished. Bailey said his farewell to the
1960s with the publication of his 'sara-
band for the sixties', *Goodbye Baby &
Amen* published in 1969. He continues to
flourish, however, and it is his energy and

tireless appetite for photography which
have carried him successfully through the
years.

With the exception of a distinctive
phase in his fashion and portrait work in
the 1960s, Bailey's photography is singularly styleless. In his fashion work, his
models are his muses. 'I'm styleless,' he
says, 'but my girls aren't.' He experiments
in many directions, with eyes constantly
inquisitive as he works in the studio or on
location, and his approach — infinitely
adaptable — seeks only the image appropriate to the context. His profession is
fashion and advertising photography, but
his natural photographic curiosity also
embraces the documentation of places
visited, things observed, 'mixed moments',
and, above all, portraiture.

When Bailey entered the world of
fashion photography, the two major
figures in the field were IRVING PENN and
RICHARD AVEDON. He acknowledges a respect for Penn, but it was from Avedon
that so many features of Bailey's early
work were derived. The blur of movement,
wide-angled distortions, tight composition
with subjects filling or even cropped within
the film frame, high-key subjects against
dead-white grounds — all were techniques
first used by Avedon. As well, the portraits
in Bailey's 1965 *Box of Pin-Ups*, owe a
debt to Avedon's *Observations* of 1959.

174 **John Lennon and
Paul McCartney**
(1965) This
photograph was
published as one of
the 36 plates in
*David Bailey's Box
of Pin-Ups*, a
series of portraits of
'the people who in
England today seem
glamorous to him'.
The tight cropping
and strong black/
white contrasts are
typical of Bailey's
picture-making
techniques. The
impact of this
portrait, however,
owes everything to
the powerful
presence of the
sitters, caught so
succinctly by the
photographer.

**High-heeled shoe
in knickers** David
Bailey has over the
last few years taken
countless photo-
graphs of his wife,
the model Marie
Helvin. This near-
abstract study has
the flawless quality
of a fashion
photograph, but, at
the same time, its
erotic implication
cannot be over-
looked.

The refreshing element Bailey brought to fashion photography was a naturalness in his models who took the place of the haughty, super-sophisticated creatures who typified the 1950s. His formula was timely, as was his discovery of the model Jean Shrimpton in 1960 when he was first under contract to *Vogue*. Through two decades the *enfant terrible* matured into the dependable professional, capable of working under incredible pressure to meet impossible deadlines.

His rupture with British *Vogue* in the 1970s – a contract which had exhausted its original vitality – the success of his fashion/gossip newspaper *Ritz*, launched in 1977, and his marriage to Marie Helvin, all marked the emergence of a new phase in Bailey's career. His fascination with photography continues unbridled. He is constantly curious about the work of other photographers and obsessively interested in equipment, conceding that he would probably be a better photographer if he stuck to one format rather than dabbling in so many techniques. At a recent count he had over 60 cameras, ranging from lightweight automatics to 10×8in plate cameras. As a rule, Bailey uses 35mm equipment on location for ease, and $2\frac{1}{4} \times 2\frac{1}{4}$in or larger formats in the studio. He always crops his photographs in the camera, using instinct, and frequently prints up his work to include the black border. He has experimented with various artificial light set-ups including ring-flash, used since the early 1960s, and strobe lights for American and British *Vogue*.

Bailey works regularly in colour but his forte is black and white photography; and within this, his most characteristic images are strong contrast studies. The grainy effect of his early work was achieved by using Tri-X at 800 ASA. He later '... went through an FP-4 phase, thinking it had more tones and less grain,' but now has gone back to Tri-X.

Tri-X may be a staunch ally, but there is not a film, lens, or camera that he has not tried, his enthusiasm undimmed. For Bailey is a survivor whose energy and drive have kept him working while the fads and popular faces he has recorded have long since faded from memory.

175

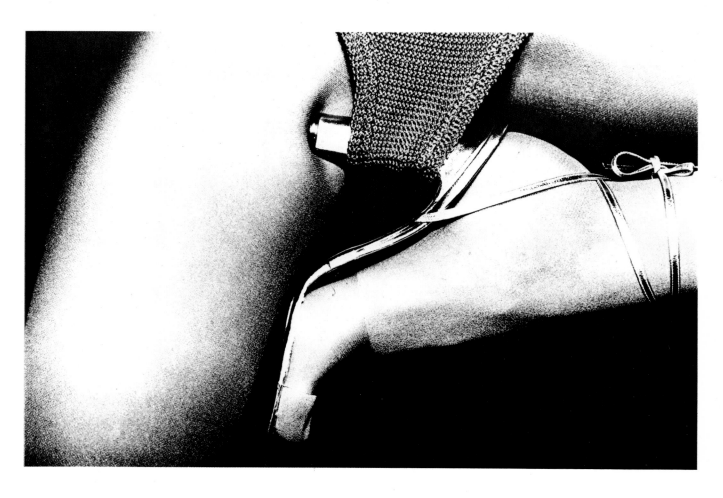

joel meyerowitz
American/born 1938

"I am most pleased when a photograph allows one to enter in, in an evenhanded way, where time can be spent, just looking."

At the beginning of his career in 1962, speed was a determining factor in Joel Meyerowitz's approach to photography. After spending an intriguing afternoon watching the Swiss photographer ROBERT FRANK work in his New York studio, within a week Meyerowitz had left his job as art director of an advertising firm, bought a 35mm hand camera, and was out on the streets of New York snapping at anything that moved. The first images were taken in colour, but these were soon replaced by black and white.

Born in 1938, and a child of the Bronx area of New York, street photography was the most natural course for Meyerowitz to pursue. 'Street-wise' from an early age, his

176   **Boy, Province-town** *(1980)*
Meyerowitz's current interest is portrait photography for which he has great enthusiasm. He takes pictures of both young and old people. This portrait of a young boy with his fish is one of his more recent photographs.

Florida *(1978)*
Between 1976 and 1978 Meyerowitz executed a series of studies on swimming pools in Florida. This particular image shows Meyerowitz's ability to use colour to its fullest extent.

St Louis and the Arch *(1977)* Meyerowitz photographed Eero Saarinen's monumental arch from many different angles. This is one of the more abstract images — an exercise in the purity of form and colour.

father had taught him not only how to defend himself physically but how to read the signs of aggression in a would-be attacker, thereby avoiding or negating a confrontation. As a photographer, this intuitive reflex enabled Meyerowitz to interpret a situation before it became manifest, and his incident photographs, shot at speeds of around 1/1000 of a second, not only manage to capture sensational moments with perfect timing, but also succeed in producing an image that is both composed and controlled.

By 1968 Meyerowitz had begun to establish himself as a prominent figure on the American photographic scene following a one-man exhibition at the Museum of Modern Art, New York, entitled 'My European Trip: Photographs from a Moving Car'. But along with his growing expertise in high-speed photography came a sense of frustration with the limitations of his aesthetic standpoint.

Although his two early mentors, Robert Frank and HENRI CARTIER-BRESSON, still maintain an influence on his work today, it was the work of the film-maker Federico Fellini who instigated the fundamental change in attitude that was gradually to revolutionize Meyerowitz's approach to photography. Meyerowitz noticed how in his films, Fellini allowed diverse images to wander loosely across the screen without making any attempt to impress them upon the viewer and thus stimulating the viewer to draw closer to the image and explore it in a random style. Clearly, this was the very opposite of what Meyerowitz had been trying to achieve in demanding the viewer's attention with a highly objective image brought out in bold relief.

By the end of the decade, Meyerowitz was steering himself in a new direction. In 1970 his experiments with colour produced a collection of colour and black and white images in a still unpublished work entitled *Going Places*, with a selection of these photographs shown at the 'Expo-70' in Japan. By 1971 colour was playing an increasingly important role in Meyerowitz's work, and he had even begun to give lessons in colour photography at the Cooper Union in New York. By 1973 he was photographing and printing almost exclusively in colour and, as his control of the medium grew, so he began to move away from incident photography and concentrate on overall field photography. This in turn brought about a new awareness of the roles of light, space and form — the latter particularly in reference to architecture.

This revolution came full cycle when in 1976 Meyerowitz bought an 8 × 10in Deardorff field view camera. This unwieldy instrument, made in 1938 and

179

weighing a healthy 45lbs, has the very unsettling complication of viewing an image both upside down and backwards which Meyerowitz has overcome by using the horizon as his 'local vertical'. He feels that by using the Deardorff with a 250mm field Ektar lens he can obtain pure results because the camera does not add sophistication to what he sees before him, either by magnifying or reducing the field of vision, thereby allowing a clear record of his own sensations to come through. The cumbersome Deardorff, with its rectilinear grid and fixed tripod, demands a certain formality in the taking of a picture and this, combined with the austerity with which Meyerowitz approachs his subject matter, produces serene images rich in subtle hues and forms.

In 1976 Meyerowitz began work on a project in the Cape Cod area near Boston, Massachusetts, with the results published in book form in 1979 as *Cape Light*. *Cape Light* unequivocally demonstrates Meyerowitz's exploration of a new aesthetic discipline. It is an impressive work that fully reveals his ability to use colour with great sensitivity and feeling.

In 1977 Meyerowitz was commissioned by the St Louis Art Museum, Missouri, to photograph Eero Saarinen's monumental Gateway Arch. The theme of these images is the pervasiveness of the Arch and, even when it appears as a reflection or an impression, the images create an effect that is both haunting and mildly claustrophobic.

In 1978, as a sequel to his work on the St Louis Arch, Meyerowitz returned to his native New York to work on another architectural project: photographing the Empire State Building. In the same year he was also a participant in 'Mirrors and Windows: American Photography since 1960', an exhibition held at the Museum of Modern Art; and in 1979 the *Cape Light* images were exhibited for the first time at the Museum of Fine Art, Boston. During this period Meyerowitz was reactivating his early interests and joined up with Colin Westerbeck to write a book on the history of street photography. He had also started working again on the streets with the 35mm camera, but this time using colour film. This was followed by a trip to China, where Meyerowitz became the first American photographer to venture up the Yangtze River.

Within two decades Meyerowitz has established a reputation in the widely divergent fields of incident and field photography. He has demonstrated his ability to master a wide range of photographic techniques and he is one of today's most versatile and exciting prospects.

180

Bay/Sky Series
(1979) In Province-
town, Cape Cod, in
1977, Meyerowitz
said that 'A color
photograph gives
you the chance to
study and remember
how things look and
feel in color. He
felt the importance
of colour in a
photograph should
not be diminished.
Meyerowitz was
back in Cape Cod
when he took this
image, in which the
orange foreground
intensifies the
already atmospheric-
ally charged
composition.

181

francis giacobetti

French-born American/born 1939

Francis Giacobetti is both a dreamer and a hard-working professional, unashamedly commercial yet with the taste and sharp eye which give his work its high quality. At a time when the photographic world is often the victim of its own pretensions, and when many photographers tread blindly in the footsteps of a few hallowed masters, high-quality commercial work comes as a breath of fresh air. Today, when black and white photography is the favoured

For Giacobetti, technique serves only as a means to an end, and most of his photographs are technically very straightforward.

medium of the 'fine art' school, colour — used joyously and boldly in a commercial context — provides a refreshing alternative.

Giacobetti has worked widely and successfully as an advertising photographer and has also been tempted by film. His reputation, however, has been earned above all as a creator of glamorized and erotic images of women, bringing vitality and fresh ideas to one of the most challenging of subjects. Giacobetti's world is a

182

controlled environment where nothing is left to chance, and in which he uses chosen elements to create an idealized vision with more than a touch of consumerist fantasy.

Francis Giacobetti was born in Marseilles, France, in 1939 and took his first photographs in 1957. Marrying young, he was forced to abandon a proposed career in law in order to earn a living. Tempted by photography, he joined *Paris Match* as a photographer's assistant, graduating to the position of photographer, but he soon realized that news photography was not for him. The realization came, he later recalled, as early as 1961 when he had been sent to cover 'the exit of John Kennedy and Charles de Gaulle from the Elysée Palace. Hundreds of photographers present were clicking wildly. I didn't make a single exposure. De Gaulle did not have the expression I would have liked, the doorway did not look right in the film frame.' Giacobetti's instinctive leaning was towards image-making rather than reportage. For Giacobetti, IRVING PENN has represented an ideal in his brilliance and integrity as an image-maker, and other, more immediate influences, were prominent American commercial photographers including, notably, Art Kane.

The subject matter that fascinated Giacobetti called for personal control of the picture-making process, and he found a

Nude, sea and sky *(1978)* The ingredients of this image have been kept to an absolute minimum. The success of the photograph owes much to its simplicity but its most remarkable quality is in the light — in the dark, almost theatrical sky, the intensity of the tropical blue/green sea, and the sparkling highlight of the crest of a breaking wave.

183

Girl swimming 185
(1974) Taken in
full sunlight using
Kodachrome 25, on
a Contax with a
60mm lens at 1/125
of a second at f.8,
this seductive image
holds no technical
secrets. Its success,
on the contrary,
derives from its
complete simplicity,
for it is the most
graphically concise
of images, tightly
composed, elimin-
ating all that is
superfluous and
exploiting a
deliberately
restricted colour
range.

186

Girl in a red dress
Giacobetti has
composed this
portrait in a limited
colour range, filling
the image with the
warm glow of the
model's red dress.
There is nothing to
distract attention
from the seductive
subject, bathing in
the warm and
romantic light.

perfect opportunity to put his talents to work as a contributor to the French magazine *Lui*, which began with the magazine's launch in 1964. *Lui* has established itself as a sophisticated vehicle for the projection of a liberated, consumerist, and glamorized life style, combining a brashness inspired by the United States with inimitable French chic. Giacobetti has been its most prolific contributor. Having developed strong links with the magazine's publisher, Publications Filipacchi, Giacobetti has been instrumental in defining the company's style.

Giacobetti has worked for other magazines as well, including *Look*, *Life*, and the stylish, now sadly defunct, German *Twen* and British *Nova*, both of which employed the most imaginative photographers through the late 1960s and early 1970s for inspired fashion and beauty features. Giacobetti has found numerous commercial patrons for advertising and promotional images, among them various airline and motor manufacturing companies. For the Italian rubber company Pirelli he conceived calendar photographs, most memorably in 1970, which won wide acclaim.

Giacobetti's skills embrace a mastery of technique which enables him to achieve the high level of quality at which he aims. But his range of techniques is kept to a deliberate minimum and never allowed to overshadow his primary skill which is the choice and preparation of his subject matter. Giacobetti's favourite camera is a Contax fitted with Zeiss lenses. Working with small format 35mm equipment for ease, he nonetheless aims at fine image quality and appreciates the high optical standards of Zeiss lenses. His requirements are satisfied by a range of five or six lenses. Anxious to avoid cluttering himself, Giacobetti shuns additional equipment, although he has used a variety of filters to good effect, most notably the gradated filters used to emphasize the dramatic beauty of tropical skies.

Giacobetti likes to use available light, often strong sunlight, and occasionally adds fill-in brightness from spotlights. His passion is for colour and slow, fine resolution film. Kodachrome II and its successor, Kodachrome 25, have been his favoured films, and he has increased their natural tendency towards rich, bright colour by deliberate underexposure, which serves to exaggerate the colour saturation. Many of his images are often composed within deliberately limited colour ranges. The relatively slow exposures to which his choice of film restricts him explains in part his fondness for the Contax which has an electromagnetic release. Giacobetti observes the world in terms of colour and, to date, has never published any work in

black and white. He relishes intense, dramatic natural light effects and, circumstances being less than ideal, has made composites of two transparencies to achieve the effects which he visualizes in his mind's eye. For Giacobetti, however, technique serves only as a means to an end, and most of his photographs are technically very straightforward. He is a master of his craft, but his real skill and talent lie in his selection of subject matter and in his ability to create images which express and invite the viewer to share in his own visual enjoyments.

Giacobetti's photographic world is defined and limited by his selective eye, the eye of an art director responsive to the symbolic beauty of the elements — both traditional and aggressively modern — of the environment. He is fascinated by the Anglo-Saxon temperament, and in the United States finds its most extreme expressions, from the traditionalism of New England to the brash modernity of Las Vegas. His visual language crystallizes a widespread fascination with the symbols of American popular culture, and with the fashionably nostalgic appeal of carefully

187

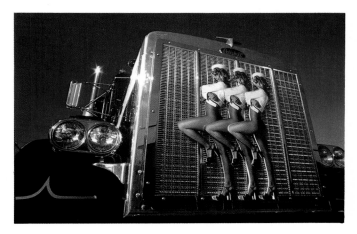

selected traditional props and settings. His most constant theme is female beauty, and his ever-youthful models parade their own charms and chic, popular fashions in contexts that are variously seductive, erotic and funky.

Giacobetti is a romantic, although his images are never sentimental. They are about the idealized look of things, reflect a sense of vitality, and are contrived with a delight in detail. American cars and trucks, gleaming chrome, flashing neon; an old brass bedstead or barber's chair, Vuitton trunks; an image of endless youth; sunlit pools, tropical beaches, luxurious villas — Giacobetti's world is the promised land of an American-styled consumer's dream, but seen through European eyes.

Truck and pin up *(1974)* This photograph is one from a series produced for *Playboy* magazine. The photographer has brought up to date in a chic pastiche the pin-ups which used to grace the radiator grilles of big trucks. He has, at the same time, paid homage to the gleaming machine with the sparkling radiator grille looming dramatically before a dense sky.

Glossary

Achromatic lens *see Lens*

Albumen paper A photographic paper plate which was coated with albumen (egg white) rather than gelatin before being sensitized.

Anastigmat lens *see Lens*

Aperture The size of the opening behind the lens which allows light into the camera so that the film is exposed. It is usually adjustable. Sometimes, it is referred to as the stop.

Aplanat lens *see Lens*

ASA A rating system which is applied to films and denotes their speed. The faster the ASA, the less time the film has to be exposed to light in order for the image to be registered.

Autochrome colour process The first practical colour process. Invented by Auguste and Louis Lumière in 1903, it incorporated a three-colour photographic plate.

B

Bromide paper A photographic printing paper which incorporates silver bromide in the emulsion with which it is coated.

Bromoil process A process whereby an oil pigment is added to a photographic print on those areas which have been washed and fixed.

C

Calotype Also called Talbotype, this was the first negative process, discovered by Fox Talbot in 1840. The negative was made from good quality paper coated with silver iodide. It was then treated with gallonitrate of silver – a mixture of gallic acid, acetic acid and silver nitrate – just before exposure. After exposure, the negative was developed by washing it in the same solution.

Camera obscura A darkened chamber into which light is admitted through a small aperture. As a result, an inverted image of the scene outside is projected onto the inside surface opposite the aperture.

Carbon process A process of making prints by contact printing onto bichromated gelatin-covered paper. The bichromate hardens on exposure to light. The unhardened gelatin layer is then washed away with water leaving a positive image on the paper. The carbro process is a variant of this, combining both the carbon and the silver bromide processes.

Carbro process *see Carbon process*

Celluloid A transparent and flexible plastic which was once used as the support for film which was coated onto it. It was used between the 1880s and the 1930s. It is a highly inflammable material and was replaced in the 1940s by non-inflammable plastics.

Collodion process A wet plate process in which collodion (a mixture of alcohol, ether, and guncotton) containing iodides was put onto a glass plate which was then submerged in silver nitrate and exposed while still wet.

Covering power The power of a lens to produce an image of acceptable sharpness over a given area of negative.

D

Daguerreotype The first commercial photographic process, discovered in 1839 and named after its inventor, Louis Daguerre (1789–1851). An image was made by exposing a copper plate coated with silver iodide. Exposures took several minutes and it was soon replaced by the wet plate process.

Diorama A miniature three-dimensional scene reproduced with the aid of lights and colours.

Dry plate process *see Wet plate process*

E

Exposure The act of exposing suitably sensitive photographic materials, such as film, glass plate or paper, to the action of light. If more or less light than is required is allowed to act on the materials they are then said to be either overexposed or underexposed. Exposure is controlled by the size of the aperture, the shutter speed and the type of film being used.

F

Fixing an image The removal by washing of unexposed silver and uneffected silver compounds during the developing of a negative so that it will not darken later when exposed to light. This makes the image permanent.

Focal plane shutter An adjustable shutter made up of one or more blinds. With this type of shutter different areas of the film are exposed at different times. When photographing objects moving at high speed the recorded image is distorted.

F. stop The aperture ring on all lenses is calibrated in a series of f. stops. These numbers denote the ratio of the diameter of the aperture to the focal length of the lens.

H

Heliogravure A former name for photogravure.

Hypo The shortened term which is used for sodium thiosulphate. Hypo is the principal chemical used for fixing.

I

Isochromatic plate An early type of plate covered with an emulsion that is sensitive to blue and green but not red light. It is similar to an orthochromatic plate.

L

Latent image An invisible chemical change takes place in photographic materials when they are exposed to light. This is when a latent or hidden image forms. It only becomes visible during development.

Lens The optical device which focuses light from an object onto the film in the camera. An achromatic lens is one which is corrected to assimilate chromatic distortions. An Aplanat or Rapid Rectilinear lens is one which corrects chromatic distortion but causes astigmatism. An anastigmat lens is one which has been corrected for astigmatism. A soft-focus lens is a lens which is specifically designed to produce photographs in which the focus is not quite sharp.

M

Multiple layer colour film A film or a plate which has several coatings of light-sensitive emulsion applied to it.

N

Negative An image of an object on either paper or film in which the range of tone (dark and light) is inverted – the lighter the object, the darker it will appear on the negative.

O

Orthochromatic plate A plate or film which is sensitive to the blue, green and yellow part of the spectrum only.

Ozobrome process A forerunner of the carbro process in which pigment prints were produced directly from bromide prints.

P

Panchromatic plate A plate or film which is sensitive to all the colours of the spectrum.

Photogram A silhouette of an object made by placing the object directly onto light-sensitive photographic paper and then exposing the paper to light.

Photogenic drawing process The first process to give fixed negatives which were made by placing objects on sensitized writing paper.

Photogravure An intaglio printing process whereby the photographic image is formed on a metal plate using a series of tiny hollows or pits. When printed, the image appears as a configuration of dots which portray light and shade.

Positive A photographic image which has tonal values which are equivalent to the scene which has been photographed. It is the opposite of a negative.

R

Rapid Rectilinear lens *see Lens*

Rangefinder The instrument which measures the distance between the lens and the object which is being photographed.

Resolution The term which is used to describe the definition of small details in a photograph. The image in which the details are well-defined is said to have 'good resolution'.

S

Sabattier effect The partial reversal of tone due to a brief exposure to light during the development of an emulsion. The results of this effect are similar to those achieved using the solarization technique.

Salted paper A early type of contact printing paper. It is made by coating paper with a solution of salt and, after drying, applying a solution of silver nitrate.

Separation negative Three negatives which, together, record the light primaries, red, green and blue.

Shutters The mechanical device on a camera which controls the time during which a film is exposed to light from the outside. They also control the size of the aperture in the camera.

Single lens reflex camera A camera with a hinged mirror which enables the photographer to view the scene in front of him on a ground glass screen in the camera.

Soft-focus lens *see Lens*

Solarization A process whereby the tonal values of a photographic image are reversed, achieved by overexposing an emulsion to light.

Stereoscope A viewer through which a stereoscopic pair of photographs is seen as a single image. The image creates the impression of three-dimensionality.

T

Talbotype *see Calotype*

Twin lens reflex camera A camera with two lenses, one placed above the other. Through the bottom lens, light is admitted to the light-sensitive film. The top lens is part of the viewfinder.

V

View camera A camera which incorporates movement so that wide-format landscape and architectural photography can be done. It is often referred to as a field or stand camera.

Viewfinder A device which is built into the camera to enable the photographer to see the field of view of the lens.

W

Wash-off relief process A means of making three-colour photographic prints by subtractive mixing of colour.

Waxed-paper negative A variation of the calotype negative. The paper is waxed before being coated with silver iodide.

Wet plate process The process which incorporated the collodion process. The plates were exposed while still wet thus requiring the photographer to prepare his plates on site. It was gradually replaced by the dry plate process. This involved coating plates with a gelatin emulsion which then dried before exposure took place.

Index

192

Acknowledgements

QED would like to thank the following for either supplying the photographs or granting permission to reproduce them or both. Unless otherwise stated, the copyright rests with the photographers themselves, to whom above all we are indebted.

Introduction: Kodak Museum, Harrow, Middlesex; Mansell Collection; Fox Talbot Museum, Lacock Abbey.
Adamson and Hill: National Portrait Gallery, London.
Le Gray: Victoria and Albert Museum, London; Bibliotèque Nationale, Paris (portrait).
Nadar: Mansell Collection (Doré); National Portrait Gallery (Rossini); Caisse Nationale des sites et monuments, Paris (portrait).
Baldus: Victoria and Albert Museum.
Watkins: International Museum of Photography, George Eastman House, New York; Weston Gallery, Carmel, California.
Carroll: National Portrait Gallery

(portrait); Rosenbach Foundation, Philadelphia; Sotheby's of Belgravia.
Cameron: National Portrait Gallery.
Muybridge: Kingston-upon-Thames Museum and Art Gallery (portrait); Victoria and Albert Museum.
Stieglitz: Metropolitan Museum of Art (portrait by Steichen).
Emerson: Robert Hershkowitz.
Atget: Caisse Nationale des sites et monuments.
Coburn: International Museum of Photography.
Steichen: Metropolitan Museum of Art; Museum of Modern Art, New York.
Sander: Shirmer Mosel Verlag GmbH, Munich.
Lartigue: Association des amis de Lartigue, Paris; Magnum (portrait by Martine Franck).
Hoppé: National Portrait Gallery; Mansell Collection.
Weston: Center for Creative Photography, Tucson, Arizona.
Strand: Paul Strand Foundation, Millerton, New York.

Evans: Collections of the Library of Congress, Washington.
Beaton: Sotheby's of Belgravia; National Portrait Gallery (portrait).
Cartier-Bresson: Magnum.
Brassaï: Museum of Modern Art; Victoria and Albert Museum; The Photographer's Gallery, London (portrait).
Brandt: portrait by John-Paul Kernot.
Adams: portrait by Gerry Sharpe.
Parkinson: portrait by Robert Pascall; by courtesy of Condé Nast Publications *(Vogue)*.
Penn: by courtesy of Condé Nast Publications *(Vogue)*.
Bailey: portrait by John Swannell, Camera Press.
QED would like to give particular thanks to all the contributors who loaned us valuable items from their private collections and also to the many photographic galleries and collections who have been so generous with their time and help in the compilation of this book.